Tudor and Stuart Texts

Early Stuart Pastoral

Tudor and Stuart Texts

Series editors

DAVID GALBRAITH
Department of English, University of Toronto

GERMAINE WARKENTIN
Department of English, University of Toronto

This is a series of modernized scholarly editions of important English Renaissance and Reformation texts, published by the Centre for Reformation and Renaissance Studies. The series emphasises texts which have not been produced in modern editions and whose availability will contribute to ongoing attempts to interpret and to teach the English Renaissance.

Titles published

The True Law of Free Monarchies and *Basilikon Doron*
JAMES I. Ed. Daniel Fischlin and Mark Fortier

The Trial of Nicholas Throckmorton
Ed. Annabel Patterson

Early Stuart Pastoral: The Shepherd's Pipe *by William Browne and others and* The Shepherd's Hunting *by George Wither*
Ed. James Doelman

For a list of CRRS publications see page 197.

Early Stuart Pastoral

The Shepherd's Pipe

by William Browne and others

and

The Shepherd's Hunting

by George Wither

Edited, with an Introduction by
James Doelman

Toronto
Centre for Reformation and Renaissance Studies
1999

CRRS Publications
Centre for Reformation and Renaissance Studies
Victoria University in the University of Toronto
Toronto, Canada M5S 1K7

Canadian Cataloguing in Publication Data

Main entry under title:

Early Stuart pastoral

(Tudor and Stuart texts)
A modernized ed.
Includes bibliographical references.
Contents: The shepherd's pipe / by William Browne and others –
The shepherd's hunting / by George Wither.
ISBN 0-9697512-9-X

1. Pastoral poetry, English. 2. English poetry – Early modern, 1500–1700.
Doelman, James Peter, 1963–   . II. Browne, William, 1590–ca. 1645.
Shepherd's pipe. III. Wither, George, 1588–1667, Shepherd;s hunting.
IV. Series.

PR1209.E27 1999   821'.408'0321734   C98-932828-7

This book has been published with the help of a grant from the Humanities
and Social Sciences Federation of Canada, using funds provided by the
Social Sciences and Humanities Research Council of Canada.

Table of Contents

Introduction

Both *The Shepherd's Pipe* (1614), by William Browne of Tavistock, Christopher Brooke, George Wither and John Davies of Hereford, and *The Shepherd's Hunting* (1615), by Wither alone, stand firmly and self-consciously within the pastoral poetic tradition.[1] They look back most directly to Spenser's *Shepheardes Calender* (1579), which in turn had partaken of a tradition stemming back through the French poet Clément Marot, and the neo-Latin Italian poets Jacopo Sannazzaro (1458–1530) and Mantuan (1448–1516).[2] All of these had found their primary model in Virgil's *Eclogues*, with which the famous Latin poet announced and began his poetic career. These poems were characterized by such common features as a rural setting, shepherds (or goatherds) as the main figures, poetry cast as dialogue, and a concern with love and the poetic vocation. Pastoral poetry as practiced by Virgil through Spenser was nearly invariably presented as the poetry of youth, simple rustic poetry upon which a poet would modestly refine his craft. A central question is repeated a number of times in the eclogues of *The Shepherd's Pipe* and *The Shepherd's Hunting*: what type of poetry should we write? All see pastoral poetry as merely preliminary or secondary to more important poetic tasks. Such poetry suited William Browne and George Wither well; both were in their early twenties and merely beginning their poetic careers. Latent in the eclogues is the suggestion that they

---

[1] Biographical information on these poets will be provided further on in this introduction.

[2] For further information on Renaissance pastoral in general, see Annabel Patterson, *Pastoral and Ideology: Virgil to Valéry*, (Berkeley: U of California P, 1987), and Sukanta Chaudhuri, *Renaissance Pastoral and its English Developments*, (Oxford: Clarendon, 1989). A modern English translation of Mantuan is found in *Adulescentia: the Eclogues of Mantuan*, ed. and trans. Lee Piepho, (New York: Garland, 1989).

will later turn to more important work, and in fact, Browne had already done so by publishing the first book of *Britannia's Pastorals*, a work far more ambitious and extensive in scope than most pastoral poetry.

In Spenser and other Renaissance poets there developed a tendency to use pastoral for political or ecclesiastical comment. The eclogues by Wither in *The Shepherd's Pipe* and *The Shepherd's Hunting* extend pastoral even further than the political and religious commentary offered by Spenser in *The Shepheardes Calender* and *Colin Clouts Come Home Again*. They present the pastoral poet banished from the traditional idyllic landscape and cast into the new role of the hunter. The "hunting" is a turn to a more satiric mode, as he lets loose his dogs to pursue the wolves that molest his flock. Wither also extends the usual bounds of pastoral verse by setting the eclogues in a cave that represents the Marshalsea prison in London. Overall, however, these changes are presented as ones only reluctantly implemented because of the persecution of the poet. In spite of this new role, Wither's eclogues confirm the pastoral ideal of Maytime festivals where poets contest for garlands woven by country lasses.

Generally, the diction of *The Shepherd's Pipe* and *The Shepherd's Hunting* is relatively simple and consistent with the pastoral form. Brooke's diction in *The Shepherd's Pipe*, Eclogue 8, is the most learned and sophisticated, that of Davies in Eclogue 10, the most rustic and archaic. That of Browne and Wither falls somewhere in between. The eclogues use a variety of verse forms, with Browne being the most experimental in this regard. Seven and eight-syllable lines are common in his poetry, and in eclogues 4, 5 and 7 he attempts long and complex stanza forms. Wither most often relies on the decasyllabic couplet, the form he had used in *Abuses Stript and Whipt*, and was to return to repeatedly in his later career. In the three new eclogues in *The Shepherd's Hunting* Roget's tale is told in these couplets, but the dialogue leading up to it takes a different form: ottava rima in the case of Eclogues 1 and 2, and a related seven-line stanza in Eclogue 3.[3]

---

[3] George Saintsbury still provides the best discussion of the prosody of Browne and Wither. See his *A History of English Prosody*, (London: MacMillan, 1908), vol. 2, pp. 117–24.

Because of their admiration for Spenser's pastoral, these poets have often been referred to as "the Spenserian poets". However, this appellation also refers to a wider group that included Michael Drayton and the brothers Phineas and Giles Fletcher, who do not obviously figure in *Shepherd's Pipe*. The poems of *The Shepherd's Pipe* imitate not only the style and subject matter of Spenser's *Shepheardes Calender*, but the very language itself. All four poets who contributed to the collection — Browne, Wither, Christopher Brooke and John Davies of Hereford — used Spenser's archaic and pseudo-archaic diction to lend an antique cast to their own work. John Davies' eclogue in particular makes use of non-standard diction; however, it is possible that some of these obscure words were still current among the rural folk in his native county of Hereford.

In the Renaissance, pastoral poetry was generally recognized as a genre in which real people and events could be "shadowed forth". As Puttenham put it in *The Arte of English Poesie*, it works "by glauncing at greater matters" under "the vaile of homely persons".[4] *The Shepheardes Calender* included glosses which, while at times ambiguous or seemingly irrelevant, provided something of a key to the eclogues. No such aids exist for *Shepherd's Pipe* and *Shepherd's Hunting*, although a few characters are identified by the dedications of the poems. The poet-figures in the eclogues are all easily identified: throughout Willie represents Browne, Roget represents Wither, Cuttie represents Brooke, and Wernocke represents John Davies of Hereford. For the other pastoral figures identification is usually less certain, but it seems likely that readers were meant to look for correspondences. In his notes to the August eclogue of *The Shepheardes Calender*, E.K. suggests that there must be a real person behind the figure Perigot, at least one "who is supposed" by most readers. Because of this precedent, readers would have been likely to approach *Shepherd's Pipe* and *Shepherd's Hunting* with the same expectations. Thus, they may have recognized the swineherd that has harmed the plain in *Shepherd's Pipe* eclogue 2, or the once-rich Neddy now brought low in eclogue 3, while for modern readers the correspondences can only be very tentative.

---

[4] (Rpt. Kent, Ohio: Kent State UP, 1970) p. 53.

The Poets

The Shepherd's Pipe is a unique collection of poetry: it is neither a solely individual work, nor like the popular anthologies of verse, such as *England's Helicon* (1600) and *England's Parnassus* (1600), compiled by an editor from disparate sources. It is the product of a group of poets, known to each other, writing eclogues which include each other as characters and which represent their poetic life together. Such "coterie" poetry was relatively common at the time, but in many circumstances it would only be circulated in manuscript and not published.[5] As it stands we cannot easily determine to what extent collaboration took place in the composing of the individual eclogues. The scholarship of the nineteenth and twentieth centuries has assigned each of the eclogues to a single author, but there is not evidence for this in all cases. Eclogue 1 in *The Shepherd's Pipe* is usually ascribed to William Browne, although the bulk of the eclogue consists of Roget, representing George Wither, retelling a tale from Hoccleve. In all the eclogues where a dialogue takes place, it is plausible that the other poets had a hand in composing the lines spoken by the characters that represent them. *The Shepherd's Hunting* differs somewhat from *The Shepherd's Pipe*, as it appeared under Wither's name alone, and depicts his particular situation more so than the eclogues of *The Shepherd's Pipe*. As he himself writes, "it altogether concerns myself", and collaborative composition seems less plausible in this case.

In addition to their admiration of Spenser, the poets who contributed to *The Shepherd's Pipe* and *The Shepherd's Hunting* seem to have shared two main connections: first, they were largely associated with the Inner Temple.[6] Secondly, they all saw themselves as standing apart from the centres of power, particularly the centre

---

[5] See Arthur Marotti, *John Donne, Coterie Poet*. Madison: U of Wisconsin P, 1986.

[6] The Inner Temple was one of the law schools of London, usually referred to collectively as the Inns of Court. These institutions were vibrant literary and cultural centres at the time, and many who attended them were never planning to actually practice law. For a detailed description of the cultural life of the Inns of Court, see Philip J. Finkelpearl, *John Marston of the Middle Temple: An Elizabethan Dramatist in His Social Setting*, (Cambridge, Mass.: Harvard UP, 1969).

represented by the royal court. Repeatedly in the two volumes their country life is depicted as threatened by outside forces.

William Browne was born about 1590 in Tavistock, Devon, and traditionally his origins have been attached to his name: he is, to most readers, William Browne of Tavistock. He attended Exeter College, Oxford, and then Clifford's Inn, another of the Inns of Court, before entering the Inner Temple about 1611. His first published poetry was an elegy on the death of Prince Henry, heir to the English throne, which appeared with one by Christopher Brooke under the title *Two Elegies* early in 1613. Later the same year the first part of Browne's major work *Britannia's Pastorals* was published. It is a work of laureate dimensions, and would have figured in Browne's career as *The Faerie Queene* did in Spenser's, and as *Poly-Olbion* did in Michael Drayton's.[7] This poem is a romance which mingles classical and rustic English pastoral figures. Throughout it celebrates not just "Britain", but the land of Tavy in particular. Browne is represented in the work by the shepherd Willie, who also appears in *The Shepherd's Pipe* and *The Shepherd's Hunting*. Unlike most pastoral poetry, *Britannia's Pastorals* is sustained by a continuing and complex plot. Browne paused before publishing the second book of *Britannia's Pastorals*, and a number of the eclogues in *The Shepherd's Pipe* concern his hesitation in producing the second book. This hesitation seems to have been brought about by envy and criticism, the traditional woes of the poet. The second book was finally published in 1616, but the third, seemingly composed in the years 1623 to 1625, was not published until the nineteenth century. While Browne did not die until 1645, he seems to have abandoned his poetic ambitions at least two decades earlier.

George Wither was of the same generation as Browne, being born in 1588. He attended Magdalen College, Oxford before moving on to the Inns of Court, entering Lincoln's Inn in 1615. By that time he had already established his reputation as a controversial poet of satiric verse. Throughout his life he held a high view of the public role of the poet. Like Browne and Brooke he wrote and published poetry on the death of Prince Henry (*Prince Henries Obsequies*,

---

[7] Drayton's *Poly-Olbion* (1612) was a vast poetic work describing the history and geography of Britain. On the place of pastoral and epic in the poetic career, see Richard Helgerson, *Self-Crowned Laureates: Spenser, Jonson, Milton and the Literary System*, (Berkeley: U of California P, 1983).

1612); this work was shortly followed by *Epithalamia* (1613), cele-
brating the marriage of Princess Elizabeth, daughter of King James,
to Frederick, Elector Palatine. Early in the same year Wither published the controversial *Abuses Stript and Whipt*, a lengthy satire on
various human vices. While he claimed, both in the work itself and
in others that followed, that he was merely castigating vice in
general, and not any particular people, readers quickly found what
they believed to be specific references in the poetry. The poem was
enormously successful, going through at least eight editions between
1613 and 1617. Eventually, the satire led to Wither's imprisonment
in the Marshalsea prison from 20 March to 26 July 1614. It was while
imprisoned that Wither composed the final eclogue of *The
Shepherd's Pipe* and eclogues one to three of *The Shepherd's Hunting*.

Allan Pritchard has convincingly argued that Wither was
imprisoned for offending Henry Howard, Earl of Northampton, who
was a powerful member of the king's privy council.[8] However, there
are many elements in *Abuses* that might have offended the king and
other powerful figures, including criticism of England's lack of
military preparedness, the poor quality and immorality of clergy,
and the rising of men of low birth to powerful positions at court.
The process by which Wither was imprisoned is not clear. A warrant
for his imprisonment in the Marshalsea is entered in the *Acts of the
Privy Council*, March 20, 1614, but there is no reference to a trial of
any sort or the reasons for the arrest. A similar entry in the *Acts of
the Privy Council* orders his release on July 10 of the same year, but
this order was countermanded four days later, and Wither was
finally released on July 26. It was during this four-month imprisonment that the majority of *The Shepherd's Hunting* was written.
During this same time Wither also composed *A Satyre: Dedicated to
His Most Excellent Majestie* (1614), in which he defends *Abuses Stript
and Whipt* and only regrets that he had not been more critical and
explicit in his satire. This work appeared in the fall of 1614.

Wither seems to have been imprisoned during the tumult preceding the 1614 Addled Parliament, and it is significant that he was
released soon after this parliament had been dispersed by order of
the king. The July 10 order for his release appears in the Privy

---

[8] "*Abuses Stript and Whipt* and Wither's Imprisonment", *Review of English
Studies*, n.s. 14 (1963): 337–45.

Council records alongside similar orders for the release of the imprisoned Christopher Neville, and bonds for discharging Sir John Saville and Sir Edwin Sandys. All three had been charged by the king with uttering seditious speeches in Parliament. The timing of Wither's imprisonment and release thus would suggest that his work was at least perceived to be connected to the agitation of what came to be known as "the Addled Parliament".

After the controversy stirred by *Abuses Stript and Whipt* Wither turned to Psalm versification and hymn-writing for a number of years, only returning to poetry of controversy with *Britains Remembrancer* in 1628. Wither continued to write poetry and some prose, nearly always political and controversial, until his death in 1667. During the Civil Wars he was an outspoken supporter of the Parliamentarians.[9]

Christopher Brooke, son of Robert Brooke, the Mayor of York, was of an earlier generation than Wither and Browne. He associated with Donne in the 1590s and early 1600s, and he was the addressee of Donne's poems "The Storm" and "The Calm". Like Browne and Wither he went through the Inns of Court. During the Addled Parliament Brooke was one of the more prominent lawyers sitting as members of the Lower House, and along with men such as Sir Edwin Sandys and John Hoskyns, zealously promoted the rights of Parliament. He published his long poem *The Ghost of Richard the Third* at this same time (it was entered in the Stationer's Register on May 15, 1614), and in this work he makes glancing criticism of the bishops and court favourites. Brooke was later to publish *A Poem on the Late Massacre in Virginia* (1622). He died in 1628.

When *The Shepherd's Pipe* was published, John Davies of Hereford had a much more firmly established poetic career than Browne, Wither or Brooke: he had begun publishing poetry in the first decade of the seventeenth century after a long career as a writing-master. Once he began publishing verse, he was quite prolific, producing numerous volumes of long, philosophical verse in such works as *Microcosmos* (1603) and *Wittes Pilgrimage* (1605). In its

---

[9] On Wither's career, see Allan Pritchard, "George Wither: the Poet as Prophet", *Studies in Philology*, 59 (1962): 211–230, Charles S. Hensley, *The Later Career of George Wither*, (The Hague: Mouton, 1969), and David Norbrook, "Levelling Poetry: George Wither and the English Revolution, 1642–1649", *English Literary Renaissance*, 21 (1991): 217–256.

pastoral setting and use of archaic language, his eclogue is quite different from anything else he published. Through his work as a writing master, he had significant contacts among the English nobility, including the Sidneys and Herberts, and he seems to have moved widely in poetic circles, numbering Donne and Jonson among his acquaintances. In the early years of the century he was writing-master at Magdalen College, at which time he may have met Wither. By 1605 he was living in London. Like all the other poets, Davies wrote verses on the death of Prince Henry (*The Muses Teares* 1613); to whom he may have earlier served as writing-master. Biographers have frequently described him as a Roman Catholic, but the evidence for this is scant. He died in 1618.

Dates of Composition and Publication

The Shepherd's Pipe was entered in the Stationer's Register on May 15, 1614; it seems likely that the eclogues were all written between the fall of 1613, when the first book of *Britannia's Pastorals* was printed, and the spring of 1614. Many of the eclogues look forward to a May festival that is approaching; this "festival" may have been a literal country festival, or a metaphoric description of a gathering based at one of the Inns of Court or taverns frequented by this group of poets. It likely would have taken place in May of 1614, and have been followed by the publication of the work. The references to Roget's imprisonment in the eclogues of *Shepherd's Hunting* clearly establish that eclogues one to three of that work were composed between March 20 and July 26 of 1614, the time of Wither's imprisonment in the Marshalsea. *Shepherd's Hunting* was entered in the Stationer's Register on Oct. 8, 1614, but not published until the following spring. In Wither's first eclogue in *Shepherd's Pipe*, there is no indication that he is writing from prison, but a section was added when he included it as eclogue five in *Shepherd's Hunting*, so that it shares the setting of the cave found in the other eclogues of that work.

Editorial Note

In establishing the text for this modernized edition I have used as a basis the first editions of both *Shepherd's Pipe* and *Shepherd's Hunting*. These first editions are closest to the historical moment which is so bound up with their content, and thus constitute the most appropriate base texts. Changes to the later editions are slight, and show no obvious input from the authors involved.

The text of *Shepherd's Pipe* is based on the 1614 edition (STC 3917), printed by Nicholas Okes for George Norton. The work was not reprinted until 1620, when it appeared in its entirety in a pirated edition of Wither's works. There are no significant changes in this second edition. For *Shepherd's Hunting* I have used as a base text the first 1615 edition printed by Thomas Snodham for George Norton (STC 25920). The second edition, also printed by Snodham in 1615, has numerous changes in punctuation, which in most cases improve the sense, and I have at times consulted this text while modernizing the punctuation. A third edition appeared in 1615, printed by W. White; this one makes no substantial changes to the text. Further editions appeared in later collections of Wither's works, including the pirated edition mentioned above, and in his *Juvenilia* of 1622 and 1626.

For those eclogues of Wither which appeared in both *Shepherd's Pipe* and *Shepherd's Hunting*, I have used the earlier *Shepherd's Pipe* version as a basis, and included the sections added in *Shepherd's Hunting* in footnotes.

Spelling of the texts has been modernized, except where doing so might alter the original pronunciation, or where there is possibility of a pun or implicit allusion. In those eclogues that use archaic or rustic language I have followed a conservative course, leaving the original spelling if it seems that a non-standard form is possibly intended. Capitalization of nouns has for the most part been omitted, except where personification or a specific reference is possible.

15

The original texts of both *Shepherd's Pipe* and *Shepherd's Hunting* make use of occasional italicizing; these have been silently eliminated except in a few cases where particular stress seems to have been the goal. Punctuation has been changed to reflect more modern usage; however, the heavier use of colons in the early modern period is still reflected.

Where space permits, archaic or obscure words have been glossed in the margins; otherwise, notes appear at the foot of the page.

Bibliography and Guide to Further Reading

Primary Works

Brooke, Christopher. *The Ghost of Richard the Third*. London: G. Eld for L. Lisle, 1614.

—————-. *A Poem on the Late Massacre in Virginia*. London, 1622.

Brooke, Christopher and William Browne. *Two Elegies, Consecrated to the Never-dying Memorie of the Most Worthily Admyred: Most Hartily Loved; and Generally Bewayled Prince; Henry Prince of Wales*. London: T. Snodham for R. More, 1613.

Browne, William. *Britannia's Pastorals*. London: T. Snodham for G. Norton, 1613.

—————. *Britannia's Pastorals. The Second Booke*. London: T. Snodham for G. Norton, 1616.

—————. *Britannia's Pastorals: A Third Book*. Ed. T. Crofton Croker. London: T. Richards, 1852.

Drayton, Michael. *Poly-Olbion*. London: H. Lownes, 1612.

Spenser, Edmund. *The Faerie Queene*. London, 1590 and 1596.

Spenser, Edmund. *The Shepheardes Calender*. London, 1579.

Wither, George. *Prince Henries Obsequies*. London: Edward Allde, 1612.

—————. *Abuses Stript, and Whipt*. London: G. Eld, 1613.

—————. *Epithalamia*. London: E. Marchant, 1613.

—————. *A Satyre: Dedicated to His Most Excellent Majestie*. London: Thomas Snodham, 1614.

—————. *Fidelia*, anonymous. London: Nicolas Okes, 1615.

—————. *A Preparation to The Psalter*. London: Nicolas Okes, 1619.

—————. *The Workes of Master George Wither*. London: John Beale for Thomas Walkley, 1620.

—————. *Faire-Virtue, the Mistresse of Phil'Aret* [anonymous]. London: John Grismond, 1622.

—————. *Juvenilia*. London: T. Snodham, 1622.

Later Editions

Brooke, Christopher. *Complete Poems*. Miscellanies of The Fuller Worthies' Library. Ed. Alexander B. Grosart. Blackburn, Lanc.: Printed for Private Circulation, 1872–6; rpt. Ann Arbor, Mich.: University Microfilms, 1979.

Browne, William. *Poems*. 2 vols. Ed. Gordon Goodwin. London: Routledge / New York: Dutton, 1894.

Davies of Hereford, John. *Complete Works*. 2 vols. Ed. Alexander B. Grosart. Edinburgh: T. & A. Constable, 1878.

Wither, George. *Miscellaneous Works*. Publications of the Spenser Society, nos. 12–13, 16, 18, 22 and 24. Manchester: C.E. Simms, 1872–78; rpt. New York: Burt Franklin, 1967.

————. *Poetry*. 2 vols. Ed. Frank Sidgwick. London: A.H. Bullen, 1902.

Selected Secondary Works

Brooks, Helen B. "John Davies of Hereford". *Dictionary of Literary Biography: Seventeenth-Century British Nondramatic Poets*. Ed. M. Thomas Hester. Detroit: Bruccoli Clark Layman, 1992.

Chaudhuri, Sukanta. *Renaissance Pastoral and its English Developments*. Oxford: Clarendon, 1989.

Doelman, James. "George Wither". *Dictionary of Literary Biography: Seventeenth-Century British Nondramatic Poets*. Ed. M. Thomas Hester. Detroit: Bruccoli Clark Layman, 1992.

Grundy, Joan. *The Spenserian Poets*. London: Arnold, 1969.

Norbrook, David. *Poetry and Politics in the English Renaissance*. London: Routledge and Kegan Paul, 1984.

Patterson, Annabel. *Pastoral and Ideology: Virgil to Valéry*. Berkeley: U of California P, 1987.

Pritchard, Allan. "George Wither: The Poet as Prophet". *Studies in Philology*, 59 (1962): 211–230.

————. "*Abuses Stript and Whipt* and Wither's Imprisonment". *Review of English Studies*. 14 (1963): 337–345.

Riddell, James A. "William Browne of Tavistock". *Dictionary of Literary Biography: Seventeenth-Century British Nondramatic Poets*. Ed. M. Thomas Hester. Detroit: Bruccoli Clark Layman, 1992.

Schabert, Ina. *Die Lyrik der Spenserianer*. Tubingen, 1977.

Tylus, Jane. "Jacobean Poetry and Lyric Disappointment" in *Soliciting Interpretation*. Ed. Elizabeth D. Harvey and Katherine E. Maus. Chicago: U of Chicago P, 1990.

THE
SHEPHEARDS
PIPE.

Τοι ποίμλω φόρμιγζ κι ἱρχαθμῶ κ̇ αὀιδη.

LONDON,
Printed by *N.O.* for *George Nor-*
ton, and are to be fold at his Shop
without Temple-barre. 1614.

The Shepherd's Pipe

Of his Friend, Master
William Browne.

A poet's born, not made:[1] no wonder then
Though Spenser, Sidney (miracles of men,
Sole English makers,[2] whose ev'n names so high
Express by implication poesy)
Were long unparalleled: for Nature, bold
In their creation, spent that precious mould,
That nobly better earth, that purer spirit,
Which poets, as their birthrights, claim t'inherit,
And in their great production, prodigal;[3]
Careless of futures,[4] well-nigh spent her all
Viewing her work: conscious sh'had suffered rack,[5]
Hath caused our countrymen e'er since to lack
That better earth, and form: long thrifty grown,

---

[1] This proverb likely goes back at least to Florus, who wrote, "Consules fiunt quotannis et novi proconsules:/Solus aut rex aut poeta non quotannis nascitur" ["Each year new consuls and proconsuls are made;/but not every year is a king or poet born"] *De Qualitate Vitae*, Fragment VIII (c. 120). It seems to have become a common Renaissance proverb; cf. Sidney's *A Defence of Poetry*, "A poet no industry can make, if his own genius be not carried into it; and therefore it is an olde proverbe, *Orator fit; poeta nascitur*" (ed. J.A. Van Dorsten, [Oxford: Oxford UP, 1966], p. 63).

[2] "Maker" had been used as a term for poet from at least the fourteenth century. See Sidney, *A Defence of Poetry*, p. 22: "I know not whether by luck or wisdom, we Englishmen have met with the Greeks in calling him a maker".

[3] *prodigal*] used as a verb here.

[4] *futures*] future events. In this sentence "careless" refers back to "nature".

[5] *rack*] destruction.

Who truly might hear poets, brought forth none:
Till now of late, seeing her stocks new-full
(By Time, and Thrift) of matter beautiful,
And quintessence of forms; what several
Our elder poets graces had,[6] those all
She now determined to unite in one,
So to surpass herself, and called him Browne.
That beggared by his birth, she's now so poor
That of true makers she can make no more.
Hereof accus'd, answer'd, she meant that he
A *species* should, no *individuum*[7] be;
That (Phoenix-like) he in himself should find
Of Poesy contained each several kind.[8]
And from this *Phoenix's* urn, thought she could take
Whereof all following Poets well to make.

    For of some form, she had now made known
    They were her errors whilst sh'intended *Browne*

In libellum, inscriptionemque.[9]

Not AEglogues your, but Eclogues to compare:[10]
Virgil's selected, yours elected are.[11]

---

   [6] *what several/Our elder poets graces had*] those graces that past poets held
separately.

   [7] *individuum*] an individual, or a member of a species.

   [8] In addition to being both parent and offspring, the phoenix was commonly
held to include in itself both sexes. See R. Van den Broek, *The Myth of the
Phoenix*, (Leiden: E.J. Brill, 1972), pp. 364–7. Van den Broek cites Zeno of
Verona, *Tract.* I, 16, 9, (*PL*, 11, 381A).

   [9] *In libellum inscriptionemque*] in libel and accusation.
By the early seventeenth century both of these terms had taken on specific legal
meanings. John Cowell, *The Interpreter* (1607) defines "libellus" as "the original
declaration of any action in the civill lawe". He does not define "inscriptio", but
OED, 6 defines the English "inscription" derived from it, as "an accusation or
challenge at law made under the condition that if it were false, the accuser would
undergo the same punishment that would have been inflicted on the accused if
found guilty".

   [10] *compare*] vie with, rival.

   [11] In these lines Johnson is alluding to the varying etymologies for the word
"eclogue", but his argument is not completely clear. The point, however, is that
Browne's poems in some way surpass Virgil's. In the Middle Ages and early

He imitates, you make: and this your creature
Expresseth well your name, and theirs, their nature.

E. Johnson[12]
Int. Temp.[13]

To the truly Virtuous,
and worthy of all Honour, the
Right Honourable EDWARD,
Lord ZOUCHE, Saint MAUR
and CANTELUPE, and one of
his M[ties], most Honourable
Privy Council.[14]

Be pleased (great Lord) when underneath the shades
Of your delightful Bramshill,[15] (where the spring

Renaissance it was commonly believed that "aeglogue" or "eglogue" was the
proper spelling, and that the word was derived from the Greek word for goat
["αἰγός"] (Helen Cooper, "The Goat and the Eclogue", *PQ* 53 (1974): 363–79).
Spenser, following Petrarch, called the twelve parts of the *The Shepheardes
Calender* "aeglogues", based on the argument that Theocritus had used goatherds as his main figures. Renaissance grammarians better versed in the classics
recognized that the word derived from ἐκλέγειν "to select", and meant that the
poems were selected as the best from a larger collection (see Chaudhuri, p. 102).
However, Johnson notes that Spenser's are "Aeglogues", thus providing another
etymology from Greek. There may also be a theological dimension: the Greek
word for divine election used in such key passages as Romans 11:5 was "ἐκλογευε".
We should not assume that Browne titles his poems "Eglogues" for the reasons
outlined by Johnson.

12 *E. Johnson*] Edward Johnson, a contemporary of Browne's at the Inner
Temple. He was not called to the bar until 1618, which suggests that he was
relatively young at the time he wrote this poem.

13 *Int. Temp.*] the Inner Temple.

14 Edward, 11th Baron Zouche of Harringworth (1556–1625) held numerous
important positions under Elizabeth and James. At the time of Browne's dedication
he was a privy councillor to James, President of the Council of Wales, member
of the Council of Virginia, and a commissioner of the treasury. Zouche is usually
given the title Lord Saint Maur and Lovel, but he he was also addressed at times
as Lord Cautelo or Cantelupe, due to his ancestors' connection to the Cauntelo
family.

15 *Bramshill*] Bramshill Manor in northeastern Hampshire was bought by Lord

Her flowers for gentle blasts with Zephyr[16] trades)
Once more to hear a silly˙ shepherd sing.[17]   ˙simple
Yours be the pleasure, mine the sonneting,
Ev'n that hath his delight, nor shall I need
To seek applause amongst the common store.
It is enough if this mine oaten reed
Please but the ear it should: I ask no more.
Nor shall those rural notes which heretofore
Your true attention graced and winged for fame
Imperfect lie;[18] Oblivion shall not gain
Aught on your worth, but sung shall be your name
So long as England yields[19] or˙ song or swain.   ˙either

  Free are my lines, though dressed in lowly state,
  And scorn to flatter but the men I hate.[20]

                              Your Honour's

                              W. BROWNE.

Zouch in 1605. He frequently entertained there.

[16] *Zephyr*] the west wind, or a mild, gentle wind.

[17] Browne had dedicated the first part of *Britannia's Pastorals* to Zouche in 1613.

[18] Browne is signalling his intention to continue and complete *Britannia's Pastorals.*

[19] *yields*] produces.

[20] This dedicatory poem is a sonnet to which a line has been added at the end of both the first and second quatrains to from a couplet. However, in both cases the added line is grammatically linked with the quatrain that follows.

Shepherd's Pipe, Eclogue 1

Introduction

This eclogue consists largely of the tale of Fortunatus as translated by Thomas Hoccleve (1370?–1450?) from the popular 14th-century collection of tales, *Gesta Romanarum*. It had not been published to that point, and Browne (or Wither) seems to have been working from the Durham Manuscript of Hoccleve's poems.[1] In the sixteenth century this manuscript was in the hands of John Stow (1525–1605), the publisher of the *Works of Chaucer* (1561). Others at the time shared Browne's interest in Hoccleve: the printer Thomas Speght, who had published the 1598 edition of Stow's Chaucer, added Hoccleve's "Balade to Henry V and the Knights of the Garter" as an appendix to the 1602 edition. About 1625 Richard James prepared a version of Hoccleve's *Remonstrance with Oldcastle*, which does not seem to have been printed.[2] Both the *Gesta Romanarum* and Hoccleve include a Christian allegorizing of the tale in prose at the end; Browne makes no reference to this treatment of the story. The inclusion of a medieval tale in the eclogue should be compared to Spenser's use of a tale he ascribes to Chaucer in February of *The Shepheardes Calender.* In his notes to that poem, however, E.K. remarks that it is "cleane in another kinde, and rather like to AEsopes fables".[3]

For the most part Browne reproduces Hoccleve's language and spelling, but in a few cases there is some modernization. Thus, he replaces "Unmeeble" with "unmoveable" (l. 99 in Furnivall), and "enow" with "enough" (l. 156); however, in other cases "enow" or

---

[1] Durham MS. Cosin V. III. 9.

[2] F. J. Furnivall, ed., *Hoccleve's Works. The Minor Poems,* (Oxford: Oxford UP, 1970), p. xliii.

[3] On sixteenth and seventeenth-century reception of Chaucer and other medieval English writers, see Alice S. Miskimin, *The Renaissance Chaucer,* (New Haven and London: Yale UP, 1975).

"ynow" is left in an archaic form.[4] Those cases in which Browne
actually substitutes a different word are given in the notes. Occasionally,
Browne omits a final pronounced ending with a resulting distortion
of rhythm: Hoccleve's "Reigned in Rome, and hadde sonnes three"
becomes "Reigned in Rome, and had sons three".

---

[4] See Jerome Mitchell, *Thomas Hoccleve: A Study in Early Fifteenth-Century English Poetic*, (Urbana: U of Illinois P, 1968), p. 130.

THE
SHEPHERD'S
PIPE.

The first Eclogue.

THE ARGUMENT.

Roget and Willie both ymet,[5]
Upon a greeny lea,[6]
With roundelays[7] and tales are set
To spend the length of day.

Willie. Roget.[8]

Willie.

Roget, droop not, see the spring
Is the earth enamelling,
And the birds on every tree
Greet this morn with melody:
Hark, how yonder throstle[9] chants it,
And her mate as proudly vaunts[10] it;
See how every stream is dressed
By her margin, with the best
Of Flora's gifts[11], she seems glad
For such brooks such flowers she had.
All the trees are quaintly[12] tired[13]
With green buds, of all desired;
And the hawthorn every day,

---

[5] *ymet*] met.

[6] *lea*] an unploughed or fallow field.

[7] *roundelayes*] simple songs, usually with a refrain.

[8] *Roget*] George Wither.

[9] *throstle*] a thrush, esp. a song-thrush or mavis.

[10] *vaunts*] boasts.

[11] *Flora*] Roman goddess of spring and flowers.

[12] *quaintly*] skillfully, elegantly.

[13] *tired*] attired.

Spreads some little shew[14] of May:
See the primrose sweetly set
By the much-loved violet
All the banks do sweetly cover,
As they would invite a lover
With his lass, to see their dressing,
And to grace them by their pressing.
Yet in all this merry tide
When all cares are laid aside,
Roget sits as if his blood
Had not felt the quick'ning good
Of the sun, nor cares to play,
Or with songs to pass the day
As he wont. Fie, Roget fly,
Raise thy head, and merrily
Tune us somewhat to thy reed:
See our flocks do freely feed,
Here we may together sit,
And for music very fit
Is this place: from yonder wood
Comes an echo shrill and good,
Twice full perfectly it will
Answer to thine oaten quill.
Roget, droop not then, but sing
Some kind welcome to the spring.

Roget

Ah Willie, Willie, why should I,
Sound my notes of jollity?
Since no sooner can I play
Any pleasing roundelay,
But some one or other still
'Gins[15] to descant on my quill;[16]
And will say, by this, he me
Meaneth in his minstrelsy.[17]

---

14 *shew*] show.

15 *'Gins*] begins.

16 *descant on my quill*] i.e. add a commentary or interpretation to his original words.

17 cf. *Abuses Stript and Whipt*, epigram 5, "To the Reader" (sig. B4v): "thou maist think (perhaps) these Satyres sting thee,/(Where onely thine owne guiltinesse doth wring thee").

If I chance to name as ass
In my song, it comes to pass,
One or other sure will take it
As his proper name, and make it
Fit to tell his nature too.[18]
Thus, whate'er I chance to do
Happens to my loss, and brings
To my name the venomed stings
Of ill report: how should I
Sound then notes of jollity?

Willie.

'Tis true indeed, we say all:
Rub a gall'd[19] horse on the gall,
Kick he will, storm and bite,
But the horse of sounder plight
Gently feels his master's hand.[20]
In the water thrust a brand
Kindled in the fire: 'twill hiss,
When a stick that taken is
From the hedge, in water thrust,
Never rokes˙ as would the first,   ˙steams
But endures the water's touch.
Roget, so it fares with such
Whose own guilt hath them enflamed,
Rage whene'er their vice is blamed.
But who in himself is free
From all spots, as lilies be,
Never stirs, do what thou can.
If thou slander such a man

---

[18] Throughout his early works Wither claimed that individuals erred in seeing themselves in the vices he satirized. By doing so they were damning themselves. However, there may be a specific allusion here to an occasion where he specifically named someone an ass by playing on the surname "Christmas": "the greatest feest i'th'yeere/And joyfullest his name at ful doth beare./A sacred syllable makes the first part;/Which since tis there alone and not in his heart:/Take it from thence with the ensuing letter,/And the remainder wil befit him better." (*Abuses Stript and Whipt* [1613], pp. 50–51). This passage was made less explicit in later editions.

[19] *galled*] sore from chafing, usually from a saddle or harness.

[20] Proverbial: "Touch (rub) a galled Horse on the back and he will wince (kick)." (Tilley, H700).

Yet he's quiet, for he knows
With him no such vices close.
Only he that is indeed
Spotted with the leperous seed
Of corrupted thoughts, and hath
An ulcerous soul in the path
Of reproof, he straight will brawl[21]
If you rub him of the gall.

Roget.[22]

But in vain then shall I keep
These my harmless flock of sheep.
And though all the day I tend them,
And from wolves and foxes shend˚ them.   ˚shield
Wicked swains that bear me spite,
In the gloomy veil of night,
Of my fold will draw the pegs,
Or else break my lambkins'˚ legs   ˚little lambs
Or unhang my wether's bell,
Or bring briers from the dell,
And them in my fold by pieces
Cast, to tangle all their fleeces.
Welladay˚ such churlish swains   ˚alas
Now and then lurk on our plains:
That I fear, a time, ere long
Shall not hear a shepherd's song,
Nor a swain shall take in task
Any wrong, nor once unmask
Such as do with vices rife
Soil the shepherd's happy life,
Except he means his sheep shall be
A prey to all their injury.
This causeth me I do no more
Chant so as I wont of yore;
Since in vain then should I keep
These my harmless flock of sheep.

---

21 *brawl*] raise a clamour.

22 No speech heading appears at this point in the 1614 edition, but clearly a change of speaker is intended.

Willie.

Yet if such thou wilt not sing,
Make the woods and vallies ring
With some other kind of lore;
Roget hath enough in store,
Sing of love, or tell some tale,
Praise the flowers, the hills, the vale.
Let us not here idle be;
Next day I will sing to thee.
Hark on knap˙ of yonder hill   ˙crest
Some sweet shepherd²³ tune his quill,
And the maidens in a round
Sit (to hear him) on the ground.
And if thou begin, shall we
Graced be with like company.
And to gird thy temples bring
Garlands for such fingering.
Then raise thee Roget.

Roget.

Gentle swain
Whom I honour for thy strain,
Though it would beseem me more
To attend thee and thy lore:
Yet lest thou might'st find in me
A neglect of courtesy,
I will sing what I did leere²⁴
Long agon˙ in Janiveere˙   ˙ago ˙January
Of a skillful aged sire,
As we toasted by the fire.

Willie.

Sing it out, it needs must be
Very good what comes from thee.

Roget.

Whilom an emperor prudent and wise,
Reigned in Rome, and had sons three,
Which he had in great chertee²⁵ and great prise;²⁶

---

23 *shepherd*] shepherds (1614).
24 *leere*] learn.

And when it shoop[27] so, that th'infirmity
Of death, which no wight may eschew or flee,
    Him threw down in his bed, he let do call
    His sons, and before him they came all.

And to the first he said in this maneere:*   *manner
"All th'eritage which at the dying
Of my father, he me left, all in fear
Leave I thee; and all that of my buying
Was with my penny, all my purchasing,
    My second son bequeath I to thee."
    And to the third son thus said he:

"Unmovable good, right none withouten* oath: *without
Thee give I may; but I to thee devise[28]
Jewels three: a ring, brooch and a cloth,
With which, and thou be guyed[29] as the wise,
Thou maist get all that ought thee suffice;
    Who so that the ring useth still to wear,
    Of all folks the love he shall conquer.

And who so the brooch beareth on his breast,
It is eke* of such virtue and such kind,   *also
That think upon what thing him liketh best,
And he as blive[30] shall it have and find,
My words son imprint well in mind:
    The cloth eke hath a marvellous nature,
    Which that shall be committed to thy cure.

Who so sit on it, if he wish where
In all the world to been, he suddenly
Without more labour shall be there.
Son those three jewels bequeath I
To thee, unto this effect certainly:
    That to study of the university
    Thou go, and that I bid and charge thee.

When he had thus said, the vexation
Of death so hasted him, that his spirit

---

25 *chertee*] affection, fondness.

26 *prise*] price, as in sense of "esteem".

27 *shoop*] past tense of "shape", in sense of "come to pass".

28 *devise*] to give by will (a legal term).

29 *guyed*] led, directed.

30 *blive*] quickly.

Anon forsook his habitation
In his body; death would no respite
Him give at all: he was of his life quit,
    And buried was with such solemnity
    As fell to his imperial dignity.

Of the youngest son I tell shall,
And speak no more of his brethren two,
For with them have I not to do at all.
Thus spake the mother Jonathas unto:
"Sin˙ God hath his will of thy father do,   ˙seeing that
    To thy father's will, would I me conform,
    And truly all his testament perform.

He three jewels, as thou knowest well,
A ring, a brooch, and a cloth thee bequeath,
Whose virtues, he thee told every deal,˙   ˙part
Or that he passed hence and yald[31] up the breath.
O good God, his departing, his death
    Full grievously sticketh unto mine heart,
    But suffered mote[32] been all how sore it smart.

In that case women have such heaviness,
That it not lieth in my cunning aright
You tell, of so great sorrow the excess;
But wise women can take it light,
And in short while put unto the flight
    All sorrow and woe, and catch again comfort;
    Now to my tale make I my resort.

"Thy father's will, my son, as I said ere,
Will I perform: have here the ring and go
To study anon, and when that thou art there,
As thy father thee bade, do even so,
And as thou wilt my blessing have also."
    She unto him as swith˙ took the ring   ˙quickly
    And bad him keep it well, for any thing.

He went unto the study general[33]
Where he got love enough, and acquaintance
Right good and friendly, the ring causing all;

---

[31] *yald*] past tense of "yield".

[32] *mote*] must.

[33] *study general*] university.

And on a day to him befell this chance,
With a woman, a morsel of pleasure
    By the streets of the university,
    As he was in his walking met he.

And right as blive˙ he had with her a tale,   ˙quickly
And therewithall sore in her love he brent;˙   ˙burned
Gay, fresh and picked˙ was she to the sale,   ˙adorned
For to that end, and to that intent
She thither came, and both forth they went.
    And he a pistle˙ round[34] in her ear,   ˙story
    Not wot I what,[35] for I ne came not there.[36]

She was his paramour, shortly to say:
This man to folks all was so lief,[37]
That they him gave abundance of money.
He feasted folks, and stood at high bonchief;[38]
Of the lack of good, he felt no grief,
    All whiles the ring he with him had;
    But failing it, his friendship gan[39] fad.˙   ˙fade

His paramour which that ycalled˙ was   ˙called
Fellicula[40], marvelled right greatly
Of the dispenses[41] of this Jonathas.
Sin˙ she no penny at all with him sy,˙   ˙since ˙saw
And on a night as there she lay him by
    In the bed, thus she to him spoke and said,
    And this petition assoil[42] him prayed.

"O reverent sir, unto whom" quoth she,
"Obey I would aye˙ with heart's humbleness,   ˙always
Since that ye han˙ had my virginity,   ˙have
You I beseech of your high gentleness,
Telleth me whence cometh the good and richess[43]

---

[34] *round*] whispered.

[35] *Not wot I what*] I know not what.

[36] *ne came not there*] did not come there.

[37] *lief*] beloved, acceptable.

[38] *bonchief*] prosperity.

[39] *gan*] began to, did.

[40] *Fellicula*] literally, "Little Poison", from the Latin, "fel, fellis", meaning gall or poison.

[41] *dispenses*] expenses, or money used to meet expenses.

[42] *assoil*] grant.

That ye with feasten folk,[44] and han[•] no store,   [•]have
By aught I see can, ne gold, ne tresore.[•]   [•]treasure

"If I tell it," quoth he, "peraventure[•]   [•]by chance
Thou wilt discover it, and out it publish;
Such is woman's inconstant nature,
They cannot keep counsel worth a rish.[45]
Better is my tongue keep, than to wish
    That I had kept close that is gone at large,
    And repentance is thing that I mote charge.[46]

"Nay, good sir," quoth she, "holdeth me not suspect;
Doubteth nothing, I can be right secre.[•]   [•]secret
Well worth were it me to been abject[•]   [•]cast out
From all good company, if I" quoth she,
"Unto you should so mistake me.
    Be not adread[•] your counsel me to shew."   [•]afraid
    "Well," said he, "thus it is at words few:

My father the ring which that thou maist see
On my finger, me at his dying day
Bequeathed, which this virtue and property
Hath: that the love of men he shall have aye[•]   [•]always
That weareth it, and there shall be no nay
    Of what thing that him liketh ask and crave,
    But with good will, he shall as blive[•] it have.   [•]quickly

Through the ring's virtuous excellence
Thus am I rich, and have ever enow.[•]"   [•]enough
"Now sir, yet a word by your licence
Suffreth me to say, and to speak now:
Is it wisdom, as that it seemeth you,
    Wear it on your finger continually?"
    "What wolst[•] thou mean," quoth he, "thereby?   [•]would

What peril thereof might there befall?"
"Right great," quoth she, "as ye in company
Walk often, fro[•] your finger might it fall,   [•]from
Or plucked off been in a ragery,[47]

---

43 *richess*] wealth.

44 *That ye with feasten folk*] that you feast people with.

45 *rish*] a rush, or stalk of the plant Juncaceae, emblematic of something of little value. Cf. the contemporary expression, "not worth a straw".

46 *charge*] overburden.

And so be lost, and that were folly.
   Take it me, let me been of it warden;
   For as my life keep it would I certain."

This Jonathas, this innocent young man,
Giving unto her words full credence,
As youth not advised best be can,
The ring her took of his insipience.   ·folly
When this was done, the heat and the fervence[48]
   Of love which he before had purchased,
   Was quenched, and love's knot was unlaced.

Men of their gifts to stint began.
"Ah," thought he, "for the ring I not ne bear,[49]
Faileth my love." "Fetch me woman"
Said he, "my ring: anon I will it wear."
She rose, and into chamber dresseth her,[50]
   And when she therein had been awhile,
   "Alas", quoth she, "out on falsehood and guile."

The chest is broken, and the ring take out,
And when he heard her complaint and cry,
He was astonied· sore, and made a shout,   ·astonished
And said: "Cursed be the day that I
Thee met first, or with mine eyne· sy.·"   ·eyes ·saw
   She wept and shewed outward cheer of woe,
   But in her heart was it nothing so.

The ring was safe enough, and in her chest
It was; all that she said was leasing,[51]
As some woman other while at best
Can lie and weep when is her liking.
This man saw her woe, and said: "Darling,
   Weep no more: God's help is nigh,"
   To him unwist· how false she was and sly.   ·unknown

He twined· thence, and home to his country   ·departed
Unto his mother the straight way he went;
And when she saw thither comen· was he,   ·come
"My son," quoth she, "what was thine intent

---

[47] *ragery*] sudden movement.
[48] *fervence*] violent emotion.
[49] *not ne bear*] do not bear. The double negative does not produce a positive.
[50] *dresseth her*] betook herself.
[51] *leasing*] lying, falsehood.

Thee, fro˙ the school, now to absent?"[52]   ˙from
   What caused thee fro˙ school hither to hie?   ˙from
   Mother, right˙ this," said he, "not would I lie,˙   ˙just

Forsooth mother, my ring is ago:˙   ˙gone
My paramour to keep I betook it,
And it is lost, for which I am full woe,
Sorrowfully unto mine heart it sit.
"Son, often have I warned thee, and yet
   For thy profit I warn thee my son:
   Unhonest women thou hereafter shun.

Thy brooch anon right woll˙ I to thee fet.˙"   ˙will ˙fetch
She brought it him, and charged him full deep
When he it took, and on his breast it set,
Bet˙ than his ring he should it keep,   ˙better
Lest he the loss bewail should and weep.
   To the university, shortly to sain˙,   ˙say
   In what he could, he hasted him again.

And when he comen˙ was, his paramour   ˙come
Him met anon, and unto her him took
As that he did erst, this young revelour;˙   ˙reveller
Her company he not a deal forsook,
Though he cause had, but, as with the hook
   Of her sleight, he before was caught and hent,˙   ˙seized
   Right so he was deceived oft[53] and blent.˙   ˙blinded

And as through virtue of the ring before
Of good he had abundance and plenty
While it was with him, or˙ he had it lore:[54]   ˙before
Right so through virtue of the brooch had he
What good him list;˙ she thought, how may this be,   ˙pleased
   Some privy thing now causeth this richess,˙   ˙wealth
   As did the ring herebefore I guess.

Wond'ring hereon she prayed him, and besought
Busily night and day, that tell he would
The cause of this; but he another thought,
He meant it close for him it kept be should,
And a long time it was or˙ he it told.   ˙before

---

[52] *absent*] withdraw.

[53] *oft*] Browne seems to have misread the original's "eft", meaning "again".

[54] *lore*] lost. Past participle of "lease", to lose.

She wept aye to and to,[55] and said: "alas,
The time and hour that ever I born was!

Trust ye not on me sir?" she said;
"Liefer* me were be slain in this place,   *rather
By that good Lord that for us all died,
Than purpose again you any fallace;[56]
Unto you would I be my life's space
  As true, as any woman in earth is
  Unto a man: doubteth nothing of this.

Small may she do, that cannot well biheet,[57]
Though not performed be such a promesse.*   *promise
This Jonathas thought her words so sweet,
That he was drunk of the pleasant sweetness
Of them, and of his foolish tenderness.
  This unto her he spake, and said tho:*   *then
  "Be of good comfort, why weepest thou so?"

And she thereto answered thus, sobbing:
"Sir" quoth she, "my heaviness and dread
Is this: I am adread* of the leesing   *afraid
Of your brooch, as almighty God forbeed*   *forbid
It happen so. Now what so God thee speed,"
  Said he: "wouldest thou in this case counsail?"[58]
  Quoth she: "that I keep it might sans fail."[59]

He said, "I have a fear and dread algate,*   *always
If I so did thou wouldst it leese*,   *lose
As thou lostest my ring, now gone but late.
"First God pray I" quoth she, "that I not cheese,*   *choose
But that my heart as the cold frost may freeze,
  Or else be it brent* with wild fire;   *burnt
  Nay, surely it to keep is my desire."

To her words credence he gave plener,[60]
And the brooch took her; and after anon,
Whereas he was before full lief* and chere*   *beloved *dear

---

[55] *to and to*] back and forth. Hoccleve uses this phrase elsewhere as well, but his examples are the only ones listed in *OED*.

[56] *fallace*] deceitfulness, trickery.

[57] *biheet*] promise.

[58] *counsail*] counsel.

[59] *sans fail*] without doubt.

[60] *plener*] full. That is, he gave her full creedence.

To folk, and had good, all was gone:
Good and friendship him lacked, there was none.
   "Woman, me fetch the brooch," quoth he, "swythee[61]
   Into thy chamber for it go, hie thee."

She into chamber went, as then he bad,˙   ˙bade
But she not brought that he sent her for;
She meant it not, but as she had be mad
Her clothes hath she all to rent and tore,
And cried: "Alas, the brooch away is bore,
   For which I wole˙ anon right with my knife   ˙will
   Myself slay: I am weary of my life.

This noise he heard, and blive˙ he to her ran,   ˙quickly
Weening[62] she would han˙ done as she spake;   ˙have
And the knife in all haste that he can
From her took, and threw it behind his back,
And said: "ne for the loss, ne for the lack[63]
   Of the brooch, sorrow not, I forgive all;
   I trust in God, that yet us help he shall.

To th'empress his mother this young man
Again him dresseth;˙ he went her unto,   ˙proceeded
And she saw him she to wonder gan;˙   ˙began
She thought: "now somewhat there is misdoe;"˙ ˙misdone
And said: "I dread thy jewels two
   Been lost now, percase[64] the brooch with the ring."
   "Mother" he said, "yea, by heaven King."

"Son, thou wotst˙ well no jewel is left   ˙knowest
Unto thee now, but the cloth precious
Which I thee take shall, thee charging eft˙   ˙again
The company of women riotous
Thou flee, lest it be to thee so grievous
   That thou it not˙ sustain shalt, ne˙ bear: ˙nor
   Such company or[65] my blessing forbear.

The cloth she fet,[66] and it hath him take;
And of his lady his mother, his leave

---

61 *swythee*] swift, quickly.

62 *weening*] supposing.

63 *ne...ne...*] neither...nor.

64 *percase*] perhaps.

65 *or*] on (1614).

66 *fet*] fetched. Browne has "felt", but this is clearly a misreading of the

He took, but first this foreward[67] gan˙ he make: ˙did
"Mother," said he, "trusteth this well and lieve,˙   ˙believe
That I shall sain,˙ for sooth ye shall it preve,˙   ˙say ˙prove
    If I leese˙ this cloth, never I your face,   ˙lose
    Henceforth see wole,˙ ne˙ you pray of grace.   ˙will ˙nor

With God's help I shall do well enow,˙   ˙enough
Her blessing he took, and to study is go;
And as before told have I unto you,
His paramour his privy mortal foe
Was wont to meet him, right even so
    She did then, and made him pleasant cheer;
    They clip˙ and kiss and walk homeward in fere.[68]   ˙embrace

When they were entered in the house, he sprad˙   ˙spread
This cloth upon the ground, and thereon sit,
And bade his paramour, this woman bad,
To sit also by him adown on it,
She doth as he commandeth, and bit;˙   ˙bade
    Had she this thought and virtue of the cloth
    Wist,[69] to han[70] set on it, had she been loath.

She for a while was full fore affesed.[71]
This Jonathas wish in his heart gan:˙   ˙did
"Would God that I might thus been eased,
That as on this cloth I and this woman
Sit here, as far were, as that never man
    Or˙ this came." And uneath[72] had he so thought,   ˙before
    But they with the cloth thither weren brought,

Right to the world's end, as that it were.
When apperceived˙ had she this, she cried   ˙noticed
As though she through girt[73] had be with a spear.
"Harrow![74] alas that ever shoop[75] this tide!

---

original's "fet".

    [67] *foreward*] covenant, promise.
    [68] *in fere*] together.
    [69] *wist*] known.
    [70] *han*] have.
    [71] *affesed*] frightened.
    [72] *unneth*] scarcely.
    [73] *girt*] struck, past participle of verb "gird".
    [74] *harrow*] a cry of distress.
    [75] *shoop*] came to pass.

How came we hither?" "Nay," he said, "abide:
   Worse is coming here, sole[76] wole[77] I thee leave
   Wild beast shallen thee devour or˙ eve.   ˙before

For thou my ring and brooch hast fro˙ me holden."   ˙from
"O reverent sir, have upon me pity,"
Quoth she, "if ye this grace do me wolden,˙   ˙will
As bring me home again to the city
Where as I this day was, but that[78] ye
   Them have again of foul death do me die;
   Your bounty on me kithe,[79] I mercy cry.

This Jonathas could nothing beware,
Ne˙ take ensample[80] of the deceits twain   ˙nor
That she did him before, but faith him bear,
And her he commanded on death's pain
Fro˙ such offences thenceforth her restrain.   ˙from
   She swore, and made thereto foreward,[81]
   But hark'neth how she bore her afterward.

When she saw and knew that the wrath and ire
That he to her had borne, was gone and past,
And all was well, the thought him eft˙ to fire;   ˙again
In her malice aye stood she steadfast,
And to enquire of him was not aghast,
   In so short time how that it might be
   That they came thither out of her country.

"Such virtue hath this cloth on which we sit,"
Said he, "that where in this world us be list,˙   ˙desired
Suddenly with the thought shallen thither fly,
And how thither come unto us unwist,˙   ˙unknown
As thing fro˙ far, unknown in the mist."   ˙from
   And therewith, to this woman fraudulent
   "To sleep" he said, "have I good talent."[82]

"Let see," quoth he, "stretch out anon thy lap,
In which wole˙ I my head down lay and rest."   ˙will

---

[76] *sole*] alone.

[77] *wole*] will.

[78] *but that*] unless.

[79] *kithe*] make known.

[80] *ensample*] deterrent, instance, practical warning.

[81] *foreward*] covenant, promise.

[82] *talent*] inclination, desire.

So was it done, and he anon gan˙ nap,   ˙did
Nap? Nay, he slept right well, at best;
What doth this woman, one the ficklest
        Of women all, but that cloth that lay
        Under him, she drew lite and lite[83] away.

Whan she it had all, "would God," quoth she,
"I were as I was this day morning!"
And therewith this root of iniquity
Had her wish, and sole˙ left him there sleeping.   ˙alone
O Jonathas! Like to thy perishing
        Art thou, thy paramour made hath thy beard,[84]
        When thou wakest, cause hast thou to be feard.˙   ˙afraid

"But thou shalt do full well, thou shalt obtain
Victory on her; thou hast done some deed
Pleasant to thy mother, well can I ween,˙   ˙surmise
For which our Lord quite˙ shall thy meed;˙   ˙repay ˙reward
And thee deliver out of thy woeful dreed.˙   ˙dread
        The child whom that the mother useth bless,[85]
        Full often sith˙ is eased in distress.   ˙afterwards

When he awoke , and neither he ne˙ fond˙   ˙nor ˙found
Woman ne˙ cloth, he wept bitterly,   ˙nor
And said, "alas, now is there in no lond˙   ˙land
Man worse I know begone[86] than am I.
On every side his look he cast, and sy˙   ˙saw
        Nothing but birds in the air flying,
        And wild beasts about him renning.˙   ˙running

Of whose sight he full sore was agrised,[87]
He thought, "all this well deserved I have:
What ailed me to be so evil advised,
That my counsel could I not keep and save?
Who can fool play? Who can mad[88] and rave?
        But he that to a woman his secree˙   ˙secret
        Discovereth: the smart cleaveth now on me."

---

83 *lite and lite*] little by little.

84 *made hath thy beard*] figurative expression: outwitted or deluded you.

85 *useth bless*] were in the custom of blessing.

86 *begone*] beset, situated. Cf. "woe-begone".

87 *agrised*] terrified, horrified.

88 *mad*] become mad, act like a madman.

He thus departeth as God would harmless,
And forth of adventure[89] his way is went.[90]
But whitherward he draw,˙ he conceitless[91]   ˙went
Was: he not knew to what place he was bent.
He passed a water which was so fervent
    That flesh upon his feet left it him none:
    All clean was departed from the bone.

It shoop˙ so that he had a little glass,   ˙chanced
Which with that water anon filled he;
And when he further in his way gone was,
Before him he beheld and saw a tree
That fair fruit bore, and in great plenty:
    He eat thereof, the taste him liked well,
    But he therethrough became a foul mesel.[92]

For which unto the ground for sorrow and woe
He fell, and said, "cursed be that day
That I was born, and time and hour also
That my mother conceived me, for aye
Now am I lost; alas and well away!"[93]
    And when some deal˙ slaked his heaviness,   ˙part
    He rose, and on his way he gan˙ him dress.   ˙did

Another water before him he sy,˙   ˙saw
Which (sore)˙ to comen in he was adrad;[94]   ˙greatly
But natheless,[95] since thereby, other way,
Ne˙ about it there could none be had,   ˙nor
He thought so straightly am I bestad,[96]
    That though it sore me affese[97] or gast,˙   ˙alarm
    Assoil[98] it wole˙ I, and through it he passed.   ˙will

And right as the first water his flesh
Departed from his feet, so the second

---

89 *of adventure*] by chance.

90 *went*] turned, changed. Past tense of "wend".

91 *conceitless*] without thought or plan.

92 *mesel*] leper.

93 cf. Job 3:3.

94 *adrad*] afraid.

95 *natheless*] nevertheless.

96 *bestad*] bestead, situated.

97 *affese*] frighten.

98 *assoil*] discharge.

Restored it, and made all whole and fresh;
And glad was he, and joyful that stoond*   *time
When he felt his feet whole were and sound.
     A vial of the water of that brook
     He filled, and fruit of the tree with him took.

Forth his journey this Jonathas held,
And as he his look about him cast;
Another tree from afar he beheld,
To which he hasted, and him hied fast.
Hungry he was, and of the fruit he thrast*   *thrust
     Into his mouth, and ate of it sadly,
     And of the lepry* he purged was thereby.   *leprosy

Of that fruit more he raught,[99] and thence is gone.
And a fair castle from afar saw he,
In compass of which, heads many one
Of men there hung, as he might well see;
But not for that he shun would, or flee.
     He thither him dresseth the straight way,
     In that ever that he can or may.

Walking so, two men came him again,[100]
And saiden thus: "dear friend, we you pray
What man be ye?" "Sirs," quoth he, "certain
A leech* I am, and though myself it say,   *doctor
Can for the health of sick folks well purvey."
     They said him: "of yonder castle the king
     A leper is, and can whole be for nothing.

"With him there hath been many a sundry leech
That undertook him well to cure and heal
On pain of their heads, but all too seech*   *sick
Their art was; 'ware that thou not with him deal,
But if thou canst the charter of health enseal,[101]
     Lest that thou leese[102] thy head, as didden they:
     But thou be wise thou find it shall no play.[103]

---

99 *raught*] reached.

100 *came him again*] came toward him in the opposite direction.

101 *enseal*] seal, close up.

102 *leese*] lose.

103 The word order here confuses the meaning: "except you be wise, you shall find it no play."

"Sirs," said he, "you thank I of your reed,˙   ˙counsel
For gently ye han˙ you to me quit:[104]   ˙have
But I not dread to lose mine heed,˙   ˙head
By God's help full safe keep I will it,
God of his grace such cunning and wit
      Hath lent me, that I hope I shall him cure;
      Full well dare I me put in adventure.[105]

They to the king's presence han˙ him lad,˙   ˙have ˙led
And him of the fruit of the second tree
He gave to eat, and bade him to be glad,
And said: "anon your health han˙ shall ye."   ˙have
Eke˙ of the second water him gave he   ˙also
      To drink, and when he those two had received
      His lepry˙ from him voided was and waived.   ˙leprosy

The King (as unto his high dignity
Convenient˙ was) gave him largely,˙suitable
And to him said: "if that it like thee
Abiden here, I more abundantly
Thee give wole."˙ "My Lord sickerly,˙"   ˙will ˙certainly
      Quoth he, "fain would I your pleasure fulfill,
      And in your high presence abide still."

"But I no while may with you abide
So mickle˙ have I to done elsewhere."   ˙much
Jonathas every day to the seaside,
Which was nigh, went, to look and enquire
If any ship drawing thither were,
      Which him home to his country lead might.
      And on a day of ships had he sight,

Well a thirty,[106] toward the castle draw,
And at time of Evensong, they all
Arriveden,˙ of which he was full faw,[107]   ˙arrived
And to the shipmen cry he gan˙ and call,   ˙began
And said: "if it so hap might and fall,
      That some of you me home to my country
      Me bring would, well quit˙ should he be;"   ˙rewarded

---

[104] *quit*] behaved.
[105] *adventure*] danger, jeopardy.
[106] *well a thirty*] "well" denotes fullness of number; thus, "a full thirty ships".
[107] *faw*] fain, glad.

And told them whither that they shoulden go.
One of the shipmen forth start at last,
And to him said: "my ship and no moe"*   *more
Of them that here been, doth shoop* and cast   *prepare
Thither to wend; let see, tell on fast,"
    Quoth the shipman, "that thou for my travail[108]
    Me give wilt, if that I thither sail.

They were accorded; Jonathas forth goeth
Unto the King to ask him licence
To twine* thence, to which the king was loath,   *depart
And nathelesse* with his benevolence,   *nevertheless
This Jonathas from his magnificence
    Departed is; and forth to the shipman
    His way he taketh, as swith* as he can.   *quickly

Into the ship he entreth, and as blive*   *quickly
As wind and weather good shoop* to be,   *happened
Thither as he purposed him arrive
They sailed forth, and came to the city
In which this serpentine woman was, she
    That had him turned with false deceitis,*   *deceits
    But where no remedy followeth, strait[109] is.

Turns been quit,* all be they good or bad,   *rewarded
Sometime, though they put been in delay.
But to my purpose: she deemed he had
Been devoured with beasts many a day
Gone, she thought he delivered was for aye.
    Folk of the city knew not Jonathas,
    So many a year was past, that he there was;

Misliking and thought changed eke his face.
Abouten* he goeth, and for his dwelling   *about
In the city, he hired him a place,
And therein exercised his cunning
Of physic, to whom weren* repairing   *were
    Many a sick wight, and all were healed;
    Well was the sick man that with him dealed.

Now shoop it[110] thus that this Fellicula,
(The well of deceivable doubleness,

---

108 *travail*] toil, trouble.
109 *strait*] difficult circumstances.
110 *shoop it*] it happened.

Follower of the steps of Dallida)[111]
Was then exalted unto high richesse,˙   ˙wealth
But she was fallen into great sickness
  And heard sain, for not might it been hid,
  How masterful a leech˙ he had him kid.[112]   ˙doctor

Messages solemn to him she sent,
Praying him to do so mickle˙ labour   ˙much
As come and see her, and he thither went.
When he her saw, that she his paramour
Had been, he well knew, and for that dettour˙   ˙debtor
  To her he was, her he thought to quite˙   ˙repay
  Or˙ he went, and no longer it respite.[113]   ˙before

But what that he was, she ne wist nat.[114]
He saw her urine, and eke˙ felt her pous,˙   ˙also ˙pulse
And said: "the sooth is this, plain and flat:
A sickness han˙ ye strange and marvellous,   ˙have
Which to avoid is wonder[115] dangerous;
  To heal you there is no way but one,
  Leech in this world other can find none.

"Adviseth you whether you list it take
Or not, for I told have you my wit."
"Ah sir," said she, "for God's sake,
That way me shew, and I shall follow it,
Whatever it be; for this sickness sit
  So nigh mine heart, that I wot˙ not how,   ˙know
  Me to demean,[116] tell on I pray yow.˙"   ˙you

"Lady ye must openly you confess,
And if against good conscience and right,
Any good han˙ ye take more or less,   ˙have
Before˙ this hour, of any manner wight,   ˙before
Yield it anon; else not in the might

---

[111] *Dallida*] Delilah, who betrayed Samson to the Philistines. This version of the name stems originally from the Septuagint. In medieval literature Delilah was frequently presented as a type of the tempting and traitorous woman.

[112] *kid*] made known.

[113] *respite*] delay.

[114] *ne wist nat*] did not know.

[115] *wonder*] wondrous.

[116] *demean*] manage, behave.

Of man is it, to give a medicine
That you may heal of your sickness and pine.[117]

If any such thing be, tell out I rede,[118]
And ye shall been all whole I you beheet;[119]
Else mine art is naught withouten dreed.'"   *dread
"O Lord", she thought, "health is a thing full sweet
Therewith desire I soverainly to meet.
    Since I it by confession may recover,
    A fool am I, but I my guilt discover."

How falsely to the son of th'Emperor
Jonathas, had she done, before them all,
As ye han* heard above, all that error   *have
Beknew[120] she, and Fellicula thee call
Well may I so, for of the bitter gall
    Thou takest the beginning of thy name,[121]
    Thou root of malice and mirror of shame.

"Then" said Jonathas, "where are those three
Jewels, that thee fro* the clerk withdrew?"   *from
"Sir, in a coffer at my bed's feet, ye
Shall find them; open it, and so pray I you."
He thought not to make it quaint[122] and tow[123]
    And say nay, and strain courtesy,
    But with right good will thither he gan* hie.   *did

The coffer he opened, and them there fond.*   *found
Who was a glad man but Jonathas, who,
The ring upon a finger of his hond*   *hand
He put, and the brooch on his breast also,
The cloth eke under his arm held he tho,*   *then
    And to her him dresseth to done his cure,
    Cure mortal, way to her sepulture.*   *burial

---

[117] *pine*] suffering, punishment, frequently mental.

[118] *I rede*] Furnivall's Hoccleve has "y rede", which makes more sense than Browne's misreading "it reed".

[119] *beheet*] promise.

[120] *Beknew*] confessed. Browne has this separated into two words, "by knew".

[121] *Fellicula*] "fel" is Latin for gall or bile.

[122] *to make it quaint*] to act proudly or haughtily.

[123] *tow*] tough. "To make it tough" is to show reluctance, be difficult. Cf. Chaucer: "He made hyt nouther towgh ne queynte." (*Book of the Duchess*, 531).

He thought rue she should, and forethink,[•]   [•]repent
That she her had unto him misbore.[•]   [•]misbehaved
And of that water her he gave to drink,
Which that his flesh from his bones before
Had twined,¹²⁴ wherethrough he was almost lore.[•]   [•]lost
    Nad[•] he relieved been, as ye above   [•]had not
    Han[•] heard, and this he did eke for her love.   [•]have

Of the fruit of the tree he gave her et,[•]   [•]eat
Which that him made into the leper start;
And blive[•] in her womb gan[•] they fret   [•]quickly [•]did
And gnaw so, that change gan her heart,
Now harkneth how it her made smart:
    Her womb opened, and out fell each entrail
    That in her was, thus it is said sans faile.¹²⁵

Thus wretchedly, lo, this guile-man died,¹²⁶
And Jonathas, with jewels three,
No longer there thought to abide,
But home to the empress his mother hasteth he;
Whereas in joy, and in prosperity
    His life led he to his dying day:
    And so God us grant that we do may.

Willie.

By my hook this is a tale
Would befit our Whitsunale:¹²⁷
Better cannot be I wist,[•]   [•]known
Descant¹²⁸ on it he that list.
And full gladly give I wold[•]   [•]would
The best cosset¹²⁹ in my fold,
And a mazer¹³⁰ for a fee,

---

124 *twined*] twisted, separated.

125 *sans faile*] without doubt.

126 *guile-man died*] Browne follows the original faithfully here. Furnivall suggests it should read: "guile-y woman died".

127 *Whitsunale*] traditional festival held in Whitsuntide, which begins seven sundays after Easter: June 12 in 1614. Writing of Elizabeth I's time, Richard Carew presented it as "a kind of faith feast, to which each contributed according to his means."

128 *Descant*] comment on.

129 *cosset*] pet lamb.

130 *mazer*] a drinking cup carved from maple wood. Cf. Spenser, *SC,* August, 26.

If this song thou'lt teachen me.
'Tis so quaint and fine a lay,
That upon our revel day
If I sung it, I might chance
(For my pains) be took to dance
With our Lady of the May.[131]

   Roget.

Roget will not say thee nay,
If thou deem'st it worth thy pains.
'Tis a song, not many swains
Singen can, and though it be
Not so decked with nicety
Of sweet words full neatly chused˙   ˙chosen
As are now by shepherds used;
Yet if well you sound the sense,
And the moral's excellence,
You shall find it quit the while,[132]
And excuse the homely style.
Well I wot,˙ the man that first   ˙know
Sung this lay, did quench his thirst,
Deeply as did ever one
In the Muses' Helicon.[133]
Many times he hath been seen
With the fairies on the green,
And to them his pipe did sound,
Whilst they dancèd in a round.
Mickle˙ solace would they make him,   ˙much
And at midnight often wake him,
And convey him from his room
To a field of yellow broom;[134]
Or into the meadows, where
Mints perfume the gentle air,
And where Flora[135] spends her treasure.
There they would begin their measure,

---

131 *Lady of the May*] the queen of the annual May festival, a traditional time of
rustic games and feasts in many parts of England at the time. In some localities
it was celebrated on May 1; in others it had become combined with Whitsunale.

132 *quit the while*] reward the time spent.

133 *Helicon*] the mount of the Muses, and the source of poetry.

134 *broom*] yellow-flowering shrub, common in pastures and on heaths.

135 *Flora*] goddess of the spring and flowers.

If it chanced night's sable shrouds
Muffled Cynthia[136] up in clouds;
Safely home, they then would see him,
And from brakes and quagmires free him.
There are few such swains as he
Nowadays for harmony.

Willie.

What was he thou praisest thus?

Roget.

Scholar unto Tityrus,[137]
Tityrus, the bravest swain
Ever livèd on the plain,
Taught him how to feed his lambs,
How to cure them, and their dams;
How to pitch the fold, and then,
How he should remove again;
Taught him when the corn was ripe,
How to make an oaten pipe;
How to join them, how to eat them,
When to open, when to shut them;
And with all the skill he had
Did instruct this willing lad.

Willie.

Happy surely was that swain!
And he was not taught in vain:
Many a one that prouder is,
Han˙ not such a song as this;   ˙have
And have garlands for their meed,˙   ˙reward
That but jar as Skelton's reed.[138]

Roget.

'Tis too true: but see the sun
Hath his journey fully run;
And his horses all in sweat,

---

136 *Cynthia*] the goddess Diana, frequently associated with the moon.

137 *Scholar unto Tityrus*] student of Tityrus. As in Spenser, *SC,* February, 92,
Tityrus represents Chaucer; the name originates in Virgil's first eclogue.

138 *Skelton's reed*] the poet John Skelton (1460?–1529).

In the ocean cool their heat;
Sever˙ we our sheep and fold them,   ˙separate
'Twill be night ere we have told them.[139]

THOMAS HOCCLEVE, one of the privy seal,[140] composed first this
tale, and was never till now imprinted. As this shall please, I may be
drawn to publish the rest of his works, being all perfect in my
hands.[141] He wrote in Chaucer's time.

---

[139] *told them*] counted them.

[140] Hoccleve was a clerk in the office of the privy seal.

[141] Peter Beal, *Index of English Literary Manuscripts*, Vol. 1, 1450–1625, (London: Mansell, 1980), notes that a manuscript of Hoccleve's *The Regement of Princes* (Ashmolean MS Br.W 258) has additions and corrections in Browne's hand. The work concerned the duty of kings, a potentially contentious topic in the heated atmosphere of early 1614.

Shepherd's Pipe, Eclogue 2

Introduction

This eclogue is based upon the opposition between "swineherds" and "shepherds", with the swineherd presented as an uncouth savage figure in contrast to the pastoral grace of the shepherds. He is not "of the plain", or "of the downs" (line 19), but an outsider who is ruining the landscape. The picture of him presented in lines 13 to 51 is of a foolish, foppish figure, ridiculously out of place at the May festival of the shepherds. It seems likely that the swineherd represents a particular poet who has attempted to join the Browne circle; however, no identification has yet been made.

Jockie is presented as a renowned poet, firmly of the pastoral world. While Davies of Hereford is represented by Wernocke in his own eclogue in the collection, it is possible that he is meant here as well. The two worlds of the swineherds and shepherds cannot be kept separate: the mutual friend Weptol introduces Jockie and the swineherd, and the swineherd attempts to infiltrate the circle of shepherd swains. "Weptol" is not a traditional pastoral name, and its awkward construction would suggest an anagram. He possibly represents John Powlet (also spelled Poulett), who at the time was a member of the Addled Parliament for Somerset.

The eclogue ends with the sense that the swineherd will be expelled, through satire if necessary. Willie's allusion to "a lad/Can hit the master-vein" of satire, is quite possibly to Wither.

THE
SHEPHERD'S
PIPE.

The second Eclogue.

THE ARGUMENT.

Two shepherds here complain the wrong
Done by a swinish lout,
That brings his hogs their sheep among,
And spoils the plain throughout.

Willie. Jockie.

Willie.

Jockie, say: what might he be
    That sits on yonder hill?
And tooteth out his notes of glee
    So uncouth and so shrill?

Jockie.

Notes of glee? bad ones I trow,˙   ˙suppose
    I have not heard beforne˙   ˙before
One so mistook˙ as Willie now: ˙mistaken
    'Tis some sow-gelder's horn.[1]
And well thou asken might'st if I
    Do know him, or from whence
He comes, that to his minstrelsy
    Requires such patience.
He is a swinward,˙ but I think   ˙swineherd
    No swinward of the best.
For much he reeketh of his swink,˙   ˙labour
    And carketh˙ for his rest.   ˙cares

---

[1] *sow-gelder's horn*] sow-gelding was a travelling occupation; the gelder would blow a horn to announce his arrival in a town. The term "sow-gelder" seems to have been frequently used as an insult: cf. Middleton, *Father Hubbard's Tale, Works,* ed. Bullen, Vol. 8, p. 73.

Willie.

Harm take the swine! What makes he here?
    What luckless planet's frowns
Have drawn him and his hogs in fear
    To root our daisied downs?
Ill mote˙ he thrive! And may his hogs   ˙might
    And all that e'er they breed,
Be ever worried by our dogs,
    For so presumptuous deed.
Why kept he not among the fens?
    Or in the copses by,
Or in the woods, and braky² glens,
    Where haws³ and acorns lie?
About the ditches of the town,
    Or hedgerows he might bring them.

Jockie.

But then some pence 'twould cost the clown
    To yoke and eke to ring them.⁴
And well I ween˙ he loves no cost   ˙know
    But what is for his back:
To go full gay him pleaseth most,
    And lets his belly lack.
Two suits he hath, the one of blue,
    The other home-spun grey:
And yet he means to make a new
    Against next revel day;
And though our May-lord⁵ at the feast
    Seemed very trimly clad,
In cloth by his own mother drest,
    Yet comes not near this lad.
His bonnet neatly on his head,
    With button on the top,
His shoes with strings of leather red,
    And stocking to his slop.⁶

---

  ² *braky*] overgrown with bushes.

  ³ *haws*] the fruit of the hawthorn tree.

  ⁴ Yoking a pig would keep it from running through hedges; putting a ring in its snout would keep it from rooting the ground.

  ⁵ *May-lord*] the mock king or lord of the May Festival.

  ⁶ *slop*] at the time "slop" could refer to either a smock or loose breeches. The

And yet for all it comes to pass,
    He not our gibing scapes:*   *escapes
Some like him to a trimmèd* ass,   *decorated
    And some to Jackanapes.[7]

Willie.

It seemeth then by what is said,
    That Jockie knows the boor;
I would my scrip[8] and hook have laid
    Thou knew'st him not before.

Jockie.

Sike* lothèd chance by fortune fell,*   *such *cruel
    (If fortune ought can do).
Not kenned him? Yes. I ken him well,
    And sometime paid for't too.

Willie.

Would Jockie ever stoop so low,
    As cognizance to take
Of sike* a churl? Full well I know   *such
    No nymph of spring or lake,
No herdess, nor no shepherd's girl,
    But fain would sit by thee,
And sea-nymphs offer shells of pearl
    For thy sweet melody.
The satyrs bring thee from the woods
    The strawberry for hire,
And all the first fruits of the bud
    To woo thee to their choir.
Silvanus'[9] songsters learn thy strain,
    For by a neighbour spring

---

latter seems to have been more common.

    [7] A "Jack-ape" is a small or half-sized domesticated ape. At some point in the sixteenth century this seems to have become "Jackanapes" and a nickname for the Duke of Suffolk, murdered in 1450.

    [8] *scrip*] shepherd's satchel.

    [9] *Silvanus*] Roman god of the wood, or uncultivated land. See Virgil, *Georgics,* 2.494, and Ovid, *Metamorphoses,* 14.639. He was frequently associated with the satyrs. He figured largely in the Renaissance pastoral tradition: see Mantuan's Fifth Eclogue and Spenser, *FQ,* I, vi.

The nightingale records again
    What thou dost primely* sing.   *originally
Nor canst thou tune a madrigal,
    Or any dreary moan,
But nymphs, or swains, or birds, or all
    Permit thee not alone.
And yet (as though devoid of these)
    Canst thou so low decline,
As leave the lovely naiads[10]
    For one that keepeth swine?
But how befell?

Jockie.

          Tother[11] day
    As to the field I set me,
Near to the Maypole on the way
    This sluggish swinward* met me.   *swineherd
And seeing Weptol with him there,
    Our fellow-swain and friend,
Bade "good day"; so on did fare
    To my proposed end.
But as back from my wint'ring ground
    I came the way before,
This rude groom all alone I found
    Stand by the alehouse door.
There was no nay[12] but I must in
    And taste a cup of ale;
Where on his pot[13] he did begin
    To stammer out a tale.
He told me how he much desired
    Th'acquaintance of us swains,
And from the forest was retired
    To graze upon our plains:
But for what cause I cannot tell,
    He can nor pipe nor sing,
Nor knows he how to dig a well,
    Nor neatly dress a spring;
Nor knows a trap nor snare to till.*   *set

---

[10] *naiads*] water-nymphs.

[11] *Tother*] the other.

[12] *There was no nay*] it could not be refused.

[13] *on his pot*] this is likely a variant on "in one's pot": to be drunk.

He sits as in a dream;
Nor scarce hath so much whistling skill
    Will hearten on a team.
Well, we so long together were,
    I gan˚ to haste a way;   ˚began
He licensed me to leave him there,
    And gave me leave to pay.

Willie.

Done like a swinward; may you all
    That close˚ with such as he,
Be used so, that gladly fall
    Into like company,
But if I fail not in mine Art,
    I'll send him to his yerd,˚   ˚yard
And make him from our plains depart
    With all his dirty herd.
I wonder he hath suffered been
    Upon our common here:
His hogs do root our younger trees
    And spoil the smelling brier.
Our purest wells they wallow in,
    All overspread with dirt,
Nor will they from our arbours lin,˚   ˚leave off
    But all our pleasures hurt.
Our curious[14] benches that we build
    Beneath a shady tree,
Shall be o'erthrown, or so defiled
    As we would loath to see.
Then join we Jockie; for the rest
    Of all our fellow swains,
I am assured will do their best
    To rid him fro˚ our plains.   ˚from

Jockie.

What is in me shall never fail
    To forward such a deed.
And sure I think we might prevail
    By some satiric reed.

---

[14] *curious*] carefully made.

Willie,

If that will do, I know a lad
    Can hit the master-vein.
But let us home, the skys are sad,
    And clouds distill in rain.

Shepherd's Pipe, Eclogue 3

Introduction

Eclogue 3 presents the story of Neddy, a once-rich swain who has been reduced to poverty through the swindling of his servants. Like the preceding eclogue this one presents a pastoral world which has been threatened or corrupted: things are no longer as they should be. Neddy cannot be positively identified: he seems to be an older poet who has fallen upon hard times, practicing his craft in a much reduced fashion: "he holy-days/In the farmers' houses plays/For his sustenance." "Neddy" was a common pet form of Edward and Edmund, and there may be a clue to his identity in the reference to "Wilkin's cote" in line 50. Thus, it may be that Neddy represents the poet Edward Wilkinson, who published the Spenserian poem *Thameseidos* in 1600 and *Isahacs Inheritance* in 1603. Unfortunately, little is known of this poet, nor whether he had any connection to Browne and his circle. One Edward Wilkinson matriculated at St. John's, Oxford ca. 1596, another in 1601.

It might also be possible that Neddy represents Edwin Sandys, a lawyer and Parliamentarian who led those opposing impositions in the 1614 Parliament. Early in 1614 there were attempts to prevent his gaining a seat, and immediately after the dissolution of the House on June 7 he was ordered not to leave London.

THE
SHEPHERD'S
PIPE

The third Eclogue.

THE ARGUMENT.

Old Neddy's poverty they moan,
Who whilom was a swain
That had more sheep himself alone,
Than ten upon the plain.

Piers.[1] Thomalin.[2]

Thomalin.

Where is every piping lad,
That the fields are not yclad
    With their milk-white sheep?
Tell me: is it holy-day,
Or is it in the month of May
    Use they long to sleep?

Piers.

Thomalin, 'tis not too late,
For the turtle˙ and her mate   ˙turtle-dove
    Sitten yet in nest:
And the throstle˙ hath not been   ˙thrush
Gath'ring worms yet on the green,
    But attends her rest.
Not a bird hath taught her young,
Nor her morning's lesson sung
    In the shady grove;

---

[1] Since at least the time of Langland, the name "Piers" had been associated in English verse with a rustic critic of the established church and court. See Norbrook, pp. 43–7. Cf. Spenser, *SC*, October.

[2] "Thomalin" was a traditional pastoral name; characters of this name appear in March and July of *The Shepheardes Calender*.

But the nightingale in dark
Singing, woke the mounting lark;
   She records her love.
Not the sun hath with his beams
Gilded yet our crystal streams
   Rising from the sea.
Mists do crown the mountain's tops,
And each pretty myrtle drops;
   'Tis but newly day.
Yet see yonder (though unwist˙)   ˙unknown
Some man cometh in the mist;
   Hast thou him beheld?
See he crosseth o'er the land
With a dog and staff in hand,
   Limping for his eld.˙   ˙age

Thomalin.

Yes, I see him, and do know him,
And we all do rev'rence owe him,
   'Tis the agèd sire
Neddy, that was wont to make
Such great feasting at the wake,[3]
   And the blessing-fire.[4]
Good old man! See how he walks:
Painful and among the balks[5]
   Picking locks of wool;
I have known the day when he
Had as much as any three,
   When their lofts were full.
Underneath yond hanging rocks
All the valley with his flocks
   Was whilom overspread:
He had milk-goats without peers,
Well-hung kine,˙ and fattened steers,   ˙cattle
   Many hundred head.
WILKINS cote[6] his Dairy was,

---

3 *wake*] this could refer to either a vigil preceding a feast-day, or an annual rural festival: in this case the latter seems more likely.

[4] A marginal note reads, "The Midsummer fires are termed so in the West parts of England." The term is not noted in the *OED*.

5 *balks*] ridges of unplowed ground.

6 *cote*] a small building for farm animals.

For a dwelling it may pass
    With the best in town.
Curds and cream with other cheer,
Have I had there in the year
    For a greeny gown.
Lasses kept it, as again
Were not fitted on the plain
    For a lusty dance:
And at parting, home would take us
Haws or sillabubs[7] to make us
    For our jovisance.˙   ˙joy
And though some in spight would tell,
Yet old Neddy took it well;
    Bidding us again
Never at his cote be strange:
Unto him that wrought this change,
    Mickle˙ be the pain!   ˙much

Piers.

What disaster, Thomalin,
This mischance hath clothed him in,
    Quickly tellen me;
Rue I do his state the more,
That he clippèd˙ heretofore   ˙embraced, held
    Some felicity.
Han˙ by night accursèd thieves   ˙have
Slain his lambs, or stolen his beeves?˙   ˙cattle
    Or consuming fire
Brent˙ his shearing-house, or stall;   ˙burned
Or a deluge drownèd all?
    Tell me it entire.
Have the winters been so set
To rain and snow, they have wet
    All his driest lair:[8]
By which means his sheep have got
Such a deadly cureless rot,
    That none living are?

---

[7] *sillabubs*] a drink made of milk curdled with wine or cider.

[8] *lair*] a bedding-place for a farm animal. Spenser used it to mean a pasture
(*Faerie Queene*, IV.viii.29.9 and 51.5).

Thomalin.

Neither waves, nor thieves, nor fire,
Nor have rots impoored[9] this Sire,
   Suretyship,[10] nor yet
Was the usurer helping on
With his damned extortion,
   Nor the chains of debt.
But deceit that ever lies
Strongest armed for treacheries
   In a bosomed friend:
That (and only that) hath brought it.
Cursèd be the head that wrought it!
   And the basest end.
Grooms he had, and he did send them
With his herds afield, to tend them,
   Had they further been;
Sluggish, lazy, thriftless elves,
Sheep had better kept themselves
   From the Fox's teen.   ˙mischief
Some would kill their sheep, and then
Bring their master home again
   Nothing but the skin;
Telling him, how in the morn
In the fold they found them torn,
   and near lying lin.[11]
If they went unto the fair
With a score of fattened ware,
   And did chance to sell,
If old Neddy had again
Half his own; I dare well sain,   ˙say
   That but seldom fell.
They at their return would say,
Such a man, or such would pay,
   Well known of your hine.[12]
Alas poor man! that subtle knave
Undid him, and vaunts it brave,[13]

---

9 *impoored*] impoverished. The *OED* lists only this instance of the word.

10 *Suretyship*] here it seems to be used to mean "certainly", but that use is not listed in *OED*; however, "surety" is used to mean "certain", "secure".

11 *lin*] flax. Wright, *English Dialect Dictionary.*

12 *hine*] farm servants or labourers.

13 *vaunts it brave*] boasts of it, glories in it. "To brave it" meant "to swagger",

Though his master pine.
Of his master he would beg
Such a lamb that broke his leg,
        And if there were none:
To the fold by night he'd bye,[14]
And them hurt full ruefully,
        Or* with staff or stone.   *either
He would have petitions new,
And for desp'rate debts would sue
        Neddy had forgot;
He would grant the other then
Tares[15] from poor and aged men,
        Or in jails they rot.
Neddy lately rich in store,
Giving much, deceived more,
        On a sudden[16] fell;
Then the steward lent him gold,
Yet no more than might be told
        Worth his master's cell.
That is gone, and all beside,
(Welladay, alack the tide).[17]
        In a hollow den,
Underneath yond gloomy wood
Wons* he now, and wails the brood   *lives
        Of ingrateful men.

Piers.

But alas! Now he is old,
Bit with hunger, nipped with cold,
        What is left him?
Or* to succour, or relieve him,   *either
Or from wants oft to reprieve him.

Thomalin.

        All's bereft him,
Save he hath a little crowd,

---

and Browne uses it in this way in *BP,* II.v.; however, here "brave" seems to be
used as an adverb, a usage not noted in *OED.*

14 *bye*] remain to linger.

15 *Tares*] vetch, cultivated as fodder for cattle.

16 *On a sudden*] suddenly.

17 Both expressions in this line mean roughly "alas".

(He in youth was of it proud)
    And a dog to dance:
With them, he holy-days
In the farmers' houses plays
    For his sustenance.

Piers.

See: he's near, let's rise and meet him,
And with dues to old age, greet him:,
    It is fitting so.

Thomalin.

'Tis a motion good and sage,
Honour still is due to age:
    Up, and let us go.

Shepherd's Pipe, Eclogue 4

Introduction

Browne's eclogue on the death of Thomas Manwood stands firmly in the tradition of the pastoral elegy, as typified by Virgil's Fifth Eclogue, and November in *The Shepheardes Calender.* Many of the usual attributes of the pastoral elegy can be found here: the autumn setting, the sympathetic response of nature, and the consolation that concludes the poem. The poem turns when Willie realizes that he is weeping for himself and his loss rather than the death of Manwood. This is the only eclogue of the two collections that is not in the form of a dialogue.

Thomas Manwood was the son of Sir Peter Manwood of Hackington in Kent, just north of Canterbury. Thomas entered the Inner Temple in 1610, and drowned in France in 1613. Outside the eclogue proper stands the poem to Manwood's sisters. Apart from the Inner Temple connection, the relationship of Browne to Manwood cannot be firmly established.

An autograph draft of this eclogue survives in a printed edition of *Britannia's Pastorals* (1616),[1] and another under the title "A pastorall Elegie on Mr. Thomas Manwood" in BL Lansdowne MS. 777, a manuscript which includes many of Browne's shorter poems.

---

[1] Salisbury Cathedral, MS T.2.45.

THE
SHEPHERD'S
PIPE

The fourth Eclogue.

THE ARGUMENT.

In this the Author bewails the death of one whom he shadoweth under the name of *Philarete*,[2] compounded of the Greek words PHILOS and ARETE, a lover of virtue, a name well-befitting him to whose memory these lines are consecrated, being sometime his truly loved (and now as much lamented) friend, Mr. Thomas Manwood, son to the worthy Sir Peter Manwood, Knight.

Under an agèd oak was Willie laid,
Willie, the lad who whilom made the rocks
To ring with joy, whilst on his pipe he played,
And from their masters wooed the neighbouring flocks;
    But now o'ercome with dolours deep
      That nigh his heart-strings rent,
    Ne˙ cared he for his silly sheep,   ˙neither
      Ne˙ cared for merriment.   ˙nor
But changed his wontèd walks
    For uncouth paths unknown,
Where none but trees might hear his plaints,
    And echo rue his moan.

Autumn it was, when drooped the sweetest flowers,
And rivers (swollen with pride) o'erlooked the banks;
Poor grew the day of summer's golden hours,
And void of sap stood Ida's[3] cedar ranks.˙   ˙rows
    The pleasant meadows sadly lay
      In chill and cooling sweats
    By rising fountains, or as they
      Feared winter's wasteful threats.

---

2 *Philarete*] this pastoral name was adopted by Wither in place of Roget in later editions of *The Shepherd's Hunting,* and in *Faire-Virtue* (1622).

    3 *Ida*] mount in Greece, where Paris was abandoned by his parents and found by shepherds; in July of *The Shepheardes Calender* it is associated with loftiness.

Against the broad-spread oak,
    Each wind in fury bears;
Yet fell their leaves not half so fast
    As did the shepherd's tears.

As was his seat, so was his gentle heart,
Meek and dejected, but his thoughts as high
As those aye-wandering lights, who both impart
Their beams on us, and heaven still beautify.
    Sad was his look, (o heavy Fate!
    That swain should be so sad
    Whose merry notes the forlorn mate
    With greatest pleasure clad.)
Broke was his tuneful pipe
    That charmed the crystal floods,
And thus his grief took airy wings
    And flew about the woods.

"Day, thou art too officious in thy place,
And night too sparing of a wishèd stay:
Ye wandering lamps: o be ye fixed a space!
Some other hemisphere grace with your ray.
    Great Phoebus![4] Daphne[5] is not here,
    Nor Hyacinthus[6] fair;
    Phoebe![7] Endimion[8] and thy dear
    Hath long since cleft the air.
But ye have surely seen
    (Whom we in sorrow miss)
A swain whom Phoebe thought her love,
    And Titan[9] deemèd his.

But he is gone; then inwards turn your light,
Behold him there; here never shall you more.
O'erhang this sad plain with eternal night!

---

[4] *Phoebus*] the god Apollo, frequently associated with the sun.

[5] *Daphne*] a nymph who rejected the love of Apollo and was turned into a laurel tree.

[6] *Hyacinthus*] a young man, renowned for his beauty, loved by Apollo. See *FQ*, III.vi.45.3 and III.xi.37.

[7] *Phoebe*] a Titaness, frequently associated with Selene.

[8] *Endimion*] beautiful young man, loved by Phoebe. See Drayton, *Endimion and Phoebe* (1595).

[9] In the sixteenth and seventeenth centuries "Titan" was used frequently as a poetic name for the sun, and thus here for Phoebus Apollo.

Or change the gaudy green she whilom wore
    To fenny black. Hyperion[10] great
      To ashy paleness turn her!
    Green well befits a lover's heat,
      But black beseems a mourner.
Yet neither this thou canst,
    or see his second birth,
His brightness blinds thine eye more now,
    Than thine did his on earth.

Let not a shepherd on our hapless plains,
Tune notes of glee, as usèd were of yore!
For Philarete is dead: let mirthful strains
With Philarete[11] cease for evermore!
    And if a fellow swain do live
      A niggard of his tears;
    The shepherdesses all will give
      To store him, part of theirs.
Or I would lend him some,
    But that the store I have
Will all be spent before I pay
    The debt I owe his grave.

O what is left can make me leave to moan!
Or what remains but doth increase it more!
Look on his sheep: alas! their master's gone.
Look on the place where we two heretofore
    With lockèd arms have vowed one love,
      (Our love which time shall see
    In shepherds' songs for evermore,
      And grace their harmony)
It solitary seems.
    Behold our flowery beds:
Their beauties fade, and violets
    For sorrow hang their heads.

'Tis not a cypress bough, a count'nance sad,
A mourning garment, wailing elegy,
A standing hearse in sable vesture clad,

---

    [10] *Hyperion*] one of the titans; his name was also frequently associated with the sun-god.

    [11] *Philarete*] the rhythm here would require that Philarete have four syllables, as it would in line 141 below. However, in the preceding line it would take only three syllables.

A tomb built to his name's eternity,
    Although the shepherds all should strive
      By yearly obsequies,
    And vow to keep thy fame alike
      In spite of destinies,
That can suppress my grief:
    All these and more may be,
Yet all in vain to recompense
    My greatest loss of thee.

Cypress may fade, the countenance be changed,
A garment rot, an elegy forgotten,
A hearse 'mongst irreligious rites be ranged,
A tomb plucked down, or else through age be rotten:
    All things th'unpartial hand of Fate
      Can raze out with a thought,
    These have a several fixèd date,
      Which ended, turn to nought.
Yet shall my truest cause
    Of sorrow firmly stay,
When these effects the wings of Time
    Shall fan and sweep away.

Look, as a sweet rose fairly budding forth
Bewrays[•] her beauties to th'enamour'd morn,   •reveals
Until some keen blast from the envious north,
Kills the sweet bud that was but newly born,
    Or else her rarest smells delighting
      Make her herself betray
    Some white and curious hand inviting
      To pluck her thence away.
So stands my mournful case;
    For had he been less good,
He yet (uncropped) had kept the stock
    Whereon he fairly stood.

Yet though so long he lived not as he might,
He had the time appointed to him given.
Who liveth but the space of one poor night,
His birth, his youth, his age is in that even.[•]   •evening
    Who ever doth the period see
      Of days by heaven forth plotted,
    Dies full of age, as well as he
      That had more years allotted.
In sad tones then, my verse
    Shall with incessant tears

Bemoan my hapless loss of him,
    And not his want of years.

In deepest passions of my grief-swoll'n breast
(Sweet soul!) this only comfort seizeth me,
That so few years should make thee so much blest,
And gave such wings to reach Eternity.
        Is this to die? No: as a ship
           Well-built, with easy wind
      A lazy hulk doth far outstrip,
          And soonest harbour find:
So Philarete fled,
    Quick was his passage given,
When others must have longer time
    To make them fit for heaven.

Then not for thee these briny tears are spent.
But as the nightingale against the brier,
'Tis for my self I moan, and do lament.
Not that thou left'st the world, but left'st me here.
        Here, where without thee all delights
           Fail of their pleasing power;
      All glorious days seem ugly nights;
          Methinks no April shower
Embroider should the earth,
    But briny tears distill,
Since Flora's[12] beauties shall no more
    Be honoured by thy quill.

And ye his sheep (in token of his lack)
Whilom* the fairest flock on all the plain: *formerly
Yeane[13] never lamb, but be it clothed in black.
Ye shady sycamores: when any swain,
        To carve his name upon your rind
          Doth come, where his doth stand,
      Shed drops, if he be so unkind
        To raze it with his hand.
And then my lovèd Muse
    No more shouldst numbers move,
But that his name should ever live,
    And after death my love.

---

12 *Flora*] goddess of flowers and spring.
13 *Yeane*] to give birth to.

This said, he sighed, and with o'er-drownèd eyes
Gazed on the heavens for what he missed on earth;
Then from the earth full sadly gan˙ arise,   ˙did
As far from future hope as present mirth.
      Unto his cote[14] with heavy pace
         As ever sorrow trode˙   ˙trod
      He went, with mind no more to trace
         Where mirthful swains abode,
And as he spent the day,
    The night he passed alone;
Was ne'er *shepherd* loved more dear,
    Nor made a truer moan.

TO THE VIRTUOUS
and much lamenting Sisters of
my ever admired friend, Mr. THOMAS
MANWOOD.

To me more known than you, is your sad chance,
Oh! had I still enjoyed such ignorance;
Then, I by these spent tears had not been known,
Nor left another's grief to sing mine own.
    Yet since his fate hath wrought these throes,
    Permit a partner in your woes
    The cause doth yield, and still may do
    Enough for you, and others too;
    But if such plaints for you are kept,
    Yet may I grieve since you have wept.
    For he more perfect grows to be
    That feels another's misery,
    And though these drops which mourning run
    From several fountains first begun
    And some far off, some nearer fleet,
    They will (at last) in one stream meet:
    Mine shall with yours, yours mix with mine,
    And make one offering at his shrine.
For whose Eternity on earth, my Muse
To build this Altar, did her best skill use;
And that you, I, and all that held him dear,
Our tears and sighs might freely offer here.

---

[14] *cote*] a small building for farm animals.

Shepherd's Pipe, Eclogue 5

Introduction

In this eclogue Willie encourages Cuttie, representing Christopher Brooke to whom the eclogue is dedicated, to give his talents greater scope by moving beyond pastoral poetry. Cuttie ought to attempt more heroic, martial verse; that is, to take the next step in the Virgilian model. Cuttie must leave the humble plains for the mountains of epic verse and the rewards of laureation that come with it. At first Cuttie resists but then agrees to "raise my subject higher than tofore"; he will first sing it to his fellow-swains at the May-festival, and get their response before venturing further.

On May 14, 1614, Brooke's *Ghost of Richard the Third* was entered in the Stationer's Register, and *The Shepherd's Pipe* the following day. This would suggest that at the time Eclogue 5 was written, Brooke had already written this more ambitious work, and Browne's eclogue is serving as an advertisement for it. Browne also supplied a commendatory poem for *The Ghost of Richard the Third*, which bears many similarities to Eclogue 5.

The eclogue has similarities to October in *The Shepheardes Calender*, where Cuddie laments the lack of support for poetry, and then points to the model of Virgil who "through his Mecoenas left his oaten reed" to turn to more heroic verse.

The narrative introduction of this eclogue is in seven-syllable couplets, but the verse form changes with the beginning of the dialogue to a decasyllabic ten-line stanza (ababbcbcdd), which reflects the influence of the Spenserian stanza. This change to a more heroic verse form comes at the very point where Roget begins to encourage Cuttie to move beyond his simple rustic verse.

THE
SHEPHERD'S
PIPE.

The fifth Eclogue.

To his ingenious[1] friend, Mr. Christopher Brooke.

THE ARGUMENT.

Willie incites his friend to write
Things of a higher fame,
Than silly shepherds use endite[2]
Veiled in a shepherd's name.

Willie and Cuttie.[3]

Morn had got the start of night,	
Lab'ring men were ready dight*	*dressed
With their shovels and their spades	
For the field, and (as their trades)	
Or at hedging wrought, or ditching	
For their food more than enriching.	
When the shepherds from the fold	
All their bleating charges told,*	*counted
And (full careful) searched if one	

---

[1] *ingenious*] The words "ingenious" and "ingenuous" were frequently confused at the time: therefore, the word used here could mean either "highly intelligent" or "natural and innocent". The commendatory poems to *The Ghost of Richard the Third* use both terms to describe Brooke: Chapman entitles his "To his Ingenuous and Much-Lov'd Friend, the Author", while Browne directs his "To His Worthy and Ingenious Friend, the Author".

[2] *use endite*] are accustomed to compose.

[3] In the February Eclogue of *The Shepheardes Calender* Cuddie is "an vnhappy Heardmans boye" who represents youth in an argument with age; in October he is presented as "the perfecte paterne of a Poete, whiche finding no maintenaunce of his state and studies, complayneth of the contempte of Poetrie, and the causes thereof". He also appears in the August eclogue.

Of all their flock were hurt or gone,
Or (if in the night-time culled)
Any had their fleeces pulled:
'Mongst the rest (not least in care)
Cuttie to his fold gan˙ fare,   ˙did
And young Willie (that had given
To his flock the latest even˙   ˙evening
Neighbourhood with Cuttie's sheep)
Shaking off refreshing sleep,
Hied him to his charge that blet;˙   ˙bleated
Where he (busied)⁴ Cuttie met.
Both their sheep told,˙ and none missed   ˙counted
Of their number; then they blissed˙   ˙blessed
Pan, and all the gods of plains,
For respecting of their trains
Of silly sheep; and in a song
Praise gave to that holy throng.
Thus they drave˙ their flocks to graze,   ˙drove
Whose white fleeces did amaze
All the lilies, as they pass
Where their usual feeding was.
Lilies angry that a creature
Of no more eye-pleasing feature
Than a sheep, by nature's duty
Should be crowned with far more beauty
Than a lily; and the power
Of white in sheep, o'ergo a flower:
From the middle of their sprout
(Like a Fury's sting)⁵ thrust out
Dart-like forks in death to steep them,
But great Pan did safely keep them;
And afforded kind repair
To their dry and wontèd lair,
Where their masters (that did eye them)
Underneath a hawthorn by them,
On their pipes thus gan˙to play,   ˙began
And with rhymes wear˙ but the day.   ˙spend

---

⁴ *busied*] engaged.

⁵The three Furies of classical mythology were spirits of avenging. They were usually represented bearing scourges or clubs. Here "sting" would mean a club or the shaft of a weapon.

Willie.

Cease Cuttie, cease, to feed these simple flocks,
And for a trumpet change thine oaten-reeds;[6]
O'erlook the vallies as aspiring rocks,
And rather march in steel, then shepherd's weeds.
Believe me Cuttie! for heroic deeds
Thy verse is fit; not for the lives of swains,
(Though both thou canst do well) and none proceeds
To leave high pitches for the lowly plains;
 Take thou a harp in hand, strive with Apollo;[7]
 Thy Muse was made to lead: then scorn to follow.

Cuttie.

Willie: to follow sheep I ne'er shall scorn;
Much less to follow any Deity;
Who 'gainst the sun (though weakened by the morn)
Would vie with looks, needeth an eagle's eye,
I dare not search the hidden mystery
Of tragic scenes; nor in a buskined style[8]
Through death and horror march, nor their height fly
Whose pens were fed with blood of this fair isle.
 It shall content me, on these happy downs
 To sing the strife for garlands, not for crowns.

Willie.

O who would not aspire, and by his wing
Keep stroke with fame, and of an earthly jar[9]
Another lesson teach the spheres to sing?
Who would a shepherd that might be a star?
See, learnèd Cuttie, on yond mountains are
Clear springs arising, and the climbing goat

---

[6] This directly echoes the beginning of Spenser's *Faerie Queene*:
 Lo I the man, whose Muse whilome did maske,
 As time her taught, in lowly Shepheards weeds,
 Am now enforst a far vnfitter taske,
 For trumpets sterne to chaunge mine Oaten reeds,
 And sing of Knights and Ladies gentle deeds;   (I. Proem. 1)
[7] *Apollo*] god of poetry and music.
[8] *buskined style*] a manner of dress associated with tragedy. Cf. *SC*, October, 113.
[9] *jar*] harsh sound, discord.

That can get up, hath water clearer far
Than when the streams do in the vallies float.
    What madman would a race by torch-light run
    That might his steps have ushered by the sun?

We shepherds tune our lays of shepherds' loves;
Or in the praise of shady groves, or springs;
We seldom hear of Cytherea's[10] doves,
Except when some more learnèd shepherd sings.
And equal meed˙ have to our sonnetings: ˙reward
A belt, a sheep-hook, or a wreath of flowers,
Is all we seek, and all our versing brings,
And more deserts than these are seldom ours.
    But thou whose muse a falcon's pitch can soar
    Mayest share the bays even with a conqueror.

Cuttie.

Why doth not Willie then produce such lines
Of men and arms as might accord with these?

Willie.

'Cause Cuttie's spirit not in Willie shines,
Pan cannot wield the Club of Hercules,
Nor dare a merlin[11] on a heron seize.
Scarce know I how to fit a shepherd's ear;
Far more unable shall I be to please
In aught, which none but semi-gods must hear;
    When by thy verse (more able) time shall see
    Thou canst give more to kings than kings to thee.

But (welladay)˙ who loves the muses now?   ˙alas
Or helps the climber of the sacred hill?
None lean to them: but strive to disallow
All heavenly dews the goddesses distill.

Willie.

Let earthly minds base muck for ever fill,
Whose music only is the chime of gold:
Deaf be their ears to each harmonious quill!
As they of learning think, so of them hold.

---

10 *Cytherea*] a Greek name of Venus.
11 *merlin*] species of small falcon.

> And if there's none deserves what thou canst do,
> Be then the poet and the patron too.[12]

I tell thee Cuttie, had I all the sheep
With thrice as many moe,˙ as on these plains   ˙more
Or shepherd or fair maiden sits to keep,
I would them all forgo, so I thy strains
Could equalize: O how our nearest swains
Do trim themselves, when on a holy-day
They haste to hear thee sing, knowing the trains
Of fairest Nymphs will come to learn thy lay.
> Well may they run and wish a parting never,
> So thy sweet tongue might charm their ears forever.

Cuttie.

These attributes (my lad) are not for me,
Bestow them where true merit hath assigned.

Willie.

And do I not, bestowing them on thee?
Believe me Cuttie, I do bear this mind,
That wheresoe'er we true deserving find,
To give a silent praise is to detract.
Obscure thy verses (more than most refined)
From any one of dullness so compact;
And rather sing to trees than to such men,
Who know not how to crown a poet's pen.

Cuttie.

Willie, by thy incitement I'll assay
To raise my subject higher than tofore,˙   ˙before
And sing it to our swains next holy-day,
Which (as approved) shall fill them with the store
Of such rare accents; if disliked, no more
Will I a higher strain than shepherds use,
But sing of woods and rivers as before.

---

[12] Brooke dedicated *The Ghost of Richard the Third* to Sir John Crompton and his wife.

Willie.

Thou wilt be ever happy in thy Muse.
    But see, the radiant sun is gotten high,
    Let's seek for shadow in the grove hereby.

Shepherd's Pipe, Eclogue 6

Introduction

In its lightness and relatively trivial subject matter Eclogue 6 differs from the others in the collection. In some ways this lightness seems to make it more likely that some allusion is intended, especially in the foolish figure of Philos, whose lunch is eaten by his dog, while he is busy bragging of it. Philos is a poet, one who used "To tune a *Hornpipe*, or a *Morrisdance*". His dog might possibly represent one of his poems, as they do in Wither's eclogues in *The Shepherd's Hunting*. Unlike the swineherd in Eclogue 2, Philos seems to be of the swains, but is still a ridiculous figure.

THE
SHEPHERD'S
PIPE.

The sixth Eclogue.

THE ARGUMENT.

Philos of his dog doth brag
    For having many feats;
The while the cur undoes his bag,
    And all his dinner eat.

Willie. Jockie.[1] Philos.

Willie.

Stay Jockie, let us rest here by this spring,
And Philos too, since we, so well are met;
This spreading oak will yield us shadowing
Till Phoebus' steeds be in the ocean wet.[2]

Jockie.

Gladly (kind swain) I yield, so thou wilt play
And make us merry with a roundelay.[3]

Philos.

No Jockie, rather wend we to the wood;
The time is fit, and filberds[4] waxen ripe,
Let's go and fray* the squirrel from his food;   *frighten
We will another time hear Willie pipe.

---

    [1] *Jockie*] there is little to indicate whether or not this is the same Jockie as in Eclogue 2.
    [2] That is, until the sun goes down.
    [3] *roundelay*] a short simple song, often danced to.
    [4] *filberds*] cultivated hazelnuts.

Willie.

But who shall keep our flocks when we are gone?
I dare not go and let them feed alone.

Jockie.

Nor I: since but the other day it fell,
Leaving my sheep to graze on yonder plain,
I went to fill my bottle at the well,
And ere I could return two lambs were slain.

Philos.

Then was thy dog ill-taught, or else asleep;
Such curs as those shall never watch my sheep.

Willie.

Yet Philos hath a dog not of the best;
He seems too lazy, and will take no pains:
More fit to lie at home and take his rest
Than catch a wand'ring sheep upon the plains.

Jockie.

'Tis true indeed: and Philos wot* ye what?   *know
I think he plays the fox[5] he grows so fat.

Philos.

Yet hath not Jockie nor yet Willie seen
A dog more nimble than is this of mine;
Nor any of the fox more heedful been
When in the shade I slept, or list to dine;
    And though I say't, hath better tricks in store
    Than both of yours, or twenty couple more.

How often have the maidens strove to take him,
When he hath crossed the plain to bark at crows!
How many lasses have I known to make him
Garlands to gird his neck, with which he goes
    Vaunting along the lands so wondrous trim,
    That not a dog of yours durst bark at him!

----

[5] *plays the fox*] dissembles in order to kill the sheep.

And when I list (as often-times I use)
To tune a Hornpipe,[6] or a Morris-dance,[7]
The dog (as he by nature could not choose)
Seeming asleep before, will leap and dance.

Willie.

Belike your dog came of a pedlar's brood,
Or Philos' music is exceeding good.

Philos.

I boast not of his kin, nor of my reed,
(Though of my reed and him I well may boast)
Yet if you will adventure that some meed*   *reward
Shall be to him that is in action most,
  As for a collar of shrill-sounding bells
  My dog shall strive with yours, or any's else.

Jockie.

Philos in truth I must confess your wag*   *rascal
(For so you call him) hath of tricks good store,
To steal the victuals from his master's bag;
More cunningly, I ne'er saw dog before.
  See Willie, see! I prithee Philos, note
  How fast thy bread and cheese goes down his throat.

Willie.

Now Philos see how mannerly your cur,
Your well-taught dog, that hath so many tricks,
Devours your dinner.

Philos.

    I wish 'twere a burr
To choke the mongrel!

Jockie.

    See how clean he licks
Your butter-box; by Pan, I do not meanly
Love Philos' dog that loves to be so cleanly.

---

 [6] *Hornpipe*] a jig-like dance.

 [7] *Morris-dance*] a costumed folk-dance.

Philos.

Well flouted,* Jockie.   *mocked

Willie.

Philos! Run amain,[8]
For in your scrip[9] he now hath thrust his head
So far, he cannot get it forth again;
See how he blindfold strags[10] along the mead;
    And at your scrip your bottle hangs, I think.
    He loves your meat, but cares not for your drink.

Jockie.

Aye, so it seems: and Philos now may go
Unto the wood, or home for other cheer.

Philos.

'Twere better he had never served me so,
Sweet meat, sour sauce, he shall aby* it deer.   *buy
    What, must he be aforehand with[11] his master?

Willie.

Only in kindness he would be your taster.

Philos.

Well Willie, you may laugh and urge my spleen;[12]
But by my hook I swear he shall it rue,
And had fared better had he fasting been.
But I must home for my allowance[13] new.
So farewell lads. Look to my fleecèd train
Till my return.

---

    [8] *amain*] with full force.

    [9] *scrip*] shepherd's bag.

    [10] *strags*] to walk with long steps, stride (from "straken"? *Middle English Dictionary*).

    [11] *be aforehand with*] take precedence over.

    [12] *spleen*] either "mirth" or "ill-humour".

    [13] *allowance*] alloted portion of food.

Jockie.

We will.

Willie.

Make haste again.

Shepherd's Pipe, Eclogue 7

Introduction

While Eclogue 7 is the last of Browne's eclogues, they do not form a series, and there is no sense of a conclusion here. The eclogue presents a conventional pastoral dispute about the honour of a woman: in this case the beautiful Phillis whom Hobbinoll plans to marry. The tone is darker than in many pastoral poems of this sort. Palinode's accusations against Phillis are serious ones: she is an unchaste woman, and the eclogue ends with Hobbinoll's threat against his fellow poet. Once again, it seems likely that the pastoral figures veil real persons. In the latter half of 1613 and first half of 1614 the most spoken of marriage was that of Frances Howard, recently divorced from the Earl of Essex, and Robert Kerr, a favorite of the king. The characterization of Phillis as an unchaste woman would certainly fit the view that many had of Frances Howard at the time. However, once again, conclusive evidence for the identification is lacking.

The eclogue is made up of inordinately long 22-line stanzas, consisting mostly of pentameter and dimeter couplets.

THE
SHEPHERD'S
PIPE.

The seventh Eclogue.

THE ARGUMENT

Palinode[1] entreats his friend
To leave a wanton lass;
Yet he pursues her to his end
And lets all counsel pass.

Palinode.   Hobbinoll.[2]

Whither wends Hobbinoll so early day?
What be thy lambkins[3] broken from the fold,
And on the plains all night have run astray?
Or are thy sheep and sheep-walks[4] both yfold?[5]
    What mister chance[6] hath brought thee to the field
    Without thy sheep? Thou wert not wont to yield
        To idle sport,
        But didst resort
As early to thy charge from drowsy bed,
As any shepherd that his flock hath fed
        Upon these downs.

Hobbinoll.

    Such heavy frowns
Fortune for others keeps, but bends on me

---

[1] *Palinode*] a traditional pastoral name; from the Latin, it means "song of recantation".

[2] *Hobbinoll*] another traditional pastoral name. In *The Shepheardes Calender*, Hobbinol represents Gabriel Harvey, and E.K. describes it as a "fained country name".

[3] *lambkins*] small lambs.

[4] *sheep-walks*] sheep pastures.

[5] *yfold*] closed.

[6] *mister chance*] sort of chance.

Smiles would befit the seat of majesty.
> Hath Palinode
> Made his abode
Upon our plains, or in some uncouth cell,
That hears not what to Hobbinoll befell?
Phillis[7] the fair, and fairer is there none,
Tomorrow must be linked in marriage bands,
'Tis I that must undo her virgin zone.[8]
Behold the man, behold the happy hands.

Palinode.

Behold the man? Nay, then the woman too,
Though both of them are very small beholding
To any power that set them on to woo.
Ah Hobbinoll! It is not worth unfolding
What shepherds say of her; thou canst not choose
But hear what language all of Phillis use;
> Yet, then such tongues,
> To her belongs
More men to sate her lust; unhappy else!
That wilt be bound to her to loose thy self.
> Forsake her first.

Hobbinoll.

> Thou most accursed!
Durst thou to slander thus the innocent,
The Graces' pattern, Virtue's president?[9]
> She, in whose eye
> Shines modesty,
Upon whose brow lust never looks with hope;
Venus ruled not in Phillis' horoscope.
'Tis not the vapour of a hemlock stem
Can spoil the perfume of sweet cinnamon;
Nor vile aspersions, or˙ by thee or them   ˙either
Cast on her name, can stay my going on.

---

7 *Phillis*] a pastoral name of long standing, being used in Virgil, Mantuan and Spenser.

8 *zone*] girdle, belt.

9 *president*] guardian, presiding deity.

Palinode.

On maist thou go, but not with such a one,
Whom (I dare swear) thou know'st is not a maid:
Remember when I met her last alone
As we to yonder grove for filberds[10] strayed,
Like to a new-struck *doe* from out the bushes,
Lacing herself, and red with gamesome˙ blushes   ˙playful
    Made towards the green,
    Loath to be seen:
And after in the grove the goatherd[11] met.
What saidst thou then? If this prevail not yet
    I'll tell thee moe.˙   ˙more
    Not long ago,
Too long I loved her, and, as thou dost now,
Would swear Diana was less chaste than she;
That Jupiter would court her, knew he how
To find a shape might tempt such chastity;
And that her thoughts were pure, as new-fall'n snow,
Or silver swans that trace the banks of Po,[12]
    And free within
    From spot of sin.
Yet like the flint her lust-swoll'n breast concealed
A hidden fire; and thus it was revealed:
    Cladon,[13] the lad
    Who whilom˙ had   ˙formerly
The Garland given for throwing best the bar,[14]
I know not by what chance or lucky star,
    Was chosen late
    To be the mate
Unto our Lady of the gleesome˙ May;[15]   ˙gleeful

---

[10] *filberds*] cultivated hazelnuts.

[11] In Renaissance pastoral, goatherds were frequently presented as negative counterparts to the Shepherd-poets. Morrell the goatherd appears in July of *The Shepheardes Calender*, E.K. adds this note: "By Gotes in scrypture be represented the wicked and reprobate, whose pastour also must needes be such." See Helen Cooper, "The Goat and the Eclogue", *PQ*, 53 (1974): 363–79.

[12] *Po*] the river of northern Italy. Cf. *Britannia's Pastorals*, I.iv.176: "As pure and simple as Albania's snow,/Or milk-white swans which stem the streams of Po".

[13] *Cladon*] possibly from the Greek "κλάδος", a young branch of a tree.

[14] *throwing the bar*] one of the games of the spring festival.

[15] See note *SP*, eclogue 1.

And was the first that danced each holy-day.
None would he take but Phillis forth to dance,
Nor any could with Phillis dance but he;
On Palinode she thenceforth not a glance
Bestows, but hates him and his poverty,
Cladon had sheep and limbs for stronger[16] load
Than e'er she saw in simple Palinode.
      He was the man
      Must clip* her then,   *embrace
For him she wreaths of flowers and chaplets[17] made,
To strawberries invites him in the shade;
      In shearing time
      And in the prime*   *spring
Would help to clip his sheep, and guard his lambs;
And at a need lend him her choicest rams;
      And on each stock
      Work such a clock[18]
With twisted coloured thread, as not a swain
On all these downs could shew the like again.
But, as it seems, the well grew dry at last,
Her fire unquenched, and she hath Cladon left;
Nor was I sorry, nor do wish to taste
The flesh whereto so many flies have cleft.
Oh Hobbinoll! Canst thou imagine she
That hath so oft been tried, so oft misdone,
Can from all other men be true to thee?
Thou knowst with me, with Cladon, she hath gone
Beyond the limits that a maiden may;
And can the name of wife those rovings stay?
      She hath not aught
      That's hid, unsought:
These eyes, these hands, so much know of that woman
As more thou canst not; can that please that's common?
      No: should I wed,
      My marriage bed,
And all that it contains, should as my heart
Be known but to myself; if we impart
      What golden rings
      The fairy brings,

---

16 *stronger*] more burdensome, oppressive.

17 *chaplets*] garlands for the head.

18 *clock*] ornamental pattern, usually used in reference to needlework.

We lose the gem, nor will they give us more.
Wives lose their value if once known before.
Behold this violet that croppèd lies:
I know not by what hand first from the stem,
With what I pluck myself shall I it prize?
I scorn the offals of a diadem;
A virgin's bed hath millions of delights.
If then good parents please she know no more;
Nor hath her servants, nor her favourites
That wait her husband's issuing at door:
She that is free both from the act and eye
Only deserves the due of Chastity.
    But Phillis is
    As far from this,
As are the poles in distance from each other:
She well beseems the daughter of her mother.
    Is there a brake
    By hill or lake
In all our plains that hath not guilty been
In keeping close her stealth? The Paphian Queen[19]
    Ne'er used her skill
    To win her will
Of young Adonis,[20] with more heart than she
Hath her allurements spent to work on me.
Leave, leave her Hobbinoll; she is so ill
That any one is good that's nought of her;
Though she be fair, the ground which oft we till
Grows with his burden old and barrener.

Hobbinoll.

With much ado, and with no little pain
Have I out-heard thy railing 'gainst my love:
But it is common, what we cannot gain
We oft disvalue; sooner shalt thou move
Yond lofty mountain from the place it stands,
Or count the meadow's flowers, or Isis'[21] sands,
    Than stir one thought
    In me that aught

---

[19] *Paphian Queen*] Venus; Paphos was a city on Cyprus where, according to some traditions, Venus was born from the waves.

[20] *Adonis*] a beautiful young man loved by Venus.

[21] *Isis' sands*] the sands of Egypt; Isis was the Egyptian nature goddess.

The Shepherd's Pipe   99

Can be in Phillis which Diana fair
And all the goddesses would not with their.
  Fond man, then cease
  To cross that peace
Which Phillis' virtue and this heart of mine
Have well begun; and for those words of thine
  I do forgive,
  If thou wilt live
Hereafter free from such reproaches moe,   `more
Since goodness never was without her foe.

Palinode.

Believe me, Hobbinoll, what I have said
Was more in love to thee than hate to her:
Think on thy liberty; let that be weighed;
Great good may oft betide if we defer
And use some short delays ere marriage rites.
Wedlock hath days of toil as joysome nights.
  Canst thou be free
  From jealousy?
Oh no: that plague will so infect thy brain
That only death must work thy peace again.
  Thou canst not dwell
  One minute well
From whence thou leav'st her; lock on her thy gate,
Yet will her mind be still adulterate.
  Not Argus'[22] eyes
  Nor ten such spies
Can make her only thine; for she will do
With those, that, shall make thee mistrust them too.

Hobbinoll.

Wilt thou not leave to taint a virgin's name?

Palinode.

A virgin? yes: as sure as is her mother.
Dost thou not hear her good report by fame?

---

[22] *Argus*] many-eyed herdsman of Greek myth.

Hobbinoll.

Fame is a liar and was never other.

Palinode.

Nay, if she ever spoke true, now she did;
And thou wilt once[23] confess what I foretold:
The fire will be disclos'd that now lies hid,
Nor will thy thought of her thus long time hold.
Yet may she (if that possible can fall)
Be true to thee that hath been false to all.

Hobbinoll.

   So pierce the rocks
   A redbreast's knocks
As the belief of aught thou tell'st me now.
Yet be my guest tomorrow.

Palinode.

     Speed your plough.
   I fear ere long
   You'll sing a song
Like that was sung hereby not long ago.
Where there is carrion never wants a crow.

Hobbinoll.

   Ill-tutored swain,
   If on the plain
Thy sheep hence-forward come where mine do feed,
They shall be sure to smart for thy misdeed.

Palinode.

Such are the thanks a friend's forewarning brings.
Now by the love I ever bore thee, stay!
Meet not mishaps! Themselves have speedy wings.

Hobbinoll.

It is in vain. Farewell. I must away.

FINIS. W.B.

---

[23] *once*] at some future time.

Shepherd's Pipe, Eclogue 8

Introduction

This eclogue by Christopher Brooke focuses exclusively on Willie and his poetic endeavours. Cuttie, representing Brooke, presents Browne as a unique poet who has combined his pastoral modesty with serious poetic endeavour. Willie is both of the humble plain and of Mount Helicon, a servant of Pan and Hermes. Willie has not simply moved from one stage on the Virgilian cycle to the next, but actually transformed the first stage, pastoral, into a higher poetic form. This eclogue serves as a companion piece to Eclogue 5 where Willie praised Cuttie's verse. The references to Browne's poetry would seem to be to his *Britannia's Pastorals,* to which Brooke had contributed a commendatory poem the previous fall.

Brooke's poetry in this passage is the most learned of any in either *The Shepherd's Pipe* or *The Shepherd's Hunting,* with references to both classical figures and contemporary philosophy. In a sense then, his own verse fulfills the ideal he recognizes in Browne's.

OTHER
ECLOGUES:

BY
Mʳ. BROOKE, Mʳ. WITHER,
and Mʳ. DAVIES.

LONDON

Printed by N.O. for G. Norton.

1614.

To his much-loved friend
Mʳ W. Browne of the
Inner Temple.D.D.[1]

Cuttie.

Willie well met, now whiles thy flocks do feed
So dangerless, and free from any fear,
Lay by thy hook, and take thy pleasant reed,
And with thy melody rebless mine ear,
 Which (upon Lammas[2] last) and on this plain,
 Thou playedst so sweetly to thy skipping train.

Willie.

Aye Cuttie, then I plain[3] unto my sheep
Notes apt for them, but far unfit for thee;
How should my lays (alas) true measure keep
With thy choice ears, or make thee melody:
 For in thy strain thou dost so far exceed,
 Thou canst not relish such my homely reed.[4]

---

[1] *D.D.*] dedicavit, "he dedicated it". Or posibly the similar phrases, "dono dedit" (he gave as a gift), or "detur ad" (let it be given to).

[2] *Lammas*] harvest festival celebrated on August 1.

[3] *plain*] complain, lament.

[4] cf. Eclogue 5, 47–56, where Willie encourages Cuttie to seek a higher strain.

Cuttie.

Thy niceness[5] shews thy cunning, nothing more,
Yet since thou seem'st so lowly in thy thought;
(Who in thy pastoral vein, and learnèd lore
Art so much praised, so far and near art sought)
    Lend me thine ears, and thou shalt hear me sing
    In praise of shepherds, and of thee their king.

My lovèd Willie, if there be a man
That never heard of a brown-coloured swan,[6]
Whose tender pinions scarcely fledged in show
Could make his way with whitest swans in Po;[7]
Or if there be among the spawn of earth,
That thinks so vilely of shepherds' birth,
That though he tune his reed in meanest key,
Yet in his brain holds not heaven, earth, and sea:
Then let him know, thou art that young brown swan,
That through the winding streams of Albion
Taking thy course, dost seem to make thy pace
With flocks full plumed equal in love and grace;
And thou art he (that through[8] thy humble strains
Do move delight to those that love the plains:)
Yet to thy self (as to thy sort) is given
A Jacob's staff,[9] to take the height of heaven;
And with a natural cosmography,
To comprehend the earth's rotundity;
Besides the working plummet[10] of thy brain,
Can sound the deeps, and secrets of the main:
For if the shepherd a true figure be
Of Contemplation (as the learn'd agree)
Which in his seeming rest, doth (restless) move
About the centre, and to heav'n above;
And in his thought is only bounded there,
Sees Nature's chain fastened to Jove's high chair;
Then thou (that art of Pan the sweetest swain

---

5 *niceness*] reserve, shyness.

6 Young swans are generally a brown or dark colour.

7 *Po*] river of northern Italy. Cf. Eclogue 6. Here the "swans" would refer to Italian poets: cf. *Colin Clouts Come Home Again,* 412.

8 *through*] though (1614).

9 *Jacob's staff*] an instrument for measuring the altitude of the sun.

10 *plummet*] a sounding-lead for measuring the depth of water.

And far transcending all his lowly train)[11]
In thy discoursive* thought, dost range as far;   *rational
Nor canst thou err, led by thine own fair star.
Thought hath no prison and the mind is free
Under the greatest king and tyranny.
Though low thou seem'st, thy Genius[12] mounts the Hill,
Where heavenly nectar doth from Jove distill,[13]
Where bays still grow (by thunder not struck down):
The Victors-Garland, and the Poets-Crown,
And underneath the Horse-foot-fount[14] doth flow,
Which gives wit verdure, and makes learning grow.
To this fair hill (from storms and tempests free)
Thou oft repair'st for Truth's discovery;
A prospect upon all times wand'ring mazes
Displaying vanity, disclosing graces;
Nay, in some cliff it leads the eye beyond
The time's horizon stripping sea and land;
And farther (not obscurely) doth divine
All future times. Here do the Muses shine,
Here dignity with safety do combine:
Pleasure with merit make a lovely twine.*   *pair
Vitam vitalem[15] they shall ever lead
That mount this hill and Learning's path do tread:
Here admiration without envy's won;
All in the light, but in the heat sit none.
And to this mount thou dost translate thine essence
Although the plains contain thy corporal presence,
Where though poor people's misery thou shew
That under griping[16] Lords they undergo,[17]
And what content they (that do lowest lie)
Receive from good-men[18] that do sit on high.

---

[11] Pan was generally thought of as the god of a lower variety of poetry than the lofty verse usually associated with Apollo.

[12] *Genius*] spirit.

[13] Helicon.

[14] *Horse-foot-fount*] Helicon, so called because it was traditionally held that it was formed by the foot of Pegasus. Cf. Spenser, *The Teares of the Muses*, 271: "The sacred springs of horsefoot Helicon".

[15] *Vitam vitalem*] a true life.

[16] *griping*] grasping, avaricious.

[17] *undergo*] are subject to, serve.

[18] *good-men*] a title of address given to those below the gentry. The rise of

And in each witty ditty (that surpasses)
Dost (for thy love) make strife 'mongst country lasses;
Yet in thy humble strain, Fame makes thee rise
And strikes thy mounting forehead 'gainst the skies.
Renowned friend: what trophy may I raise
To memorize thy name? Would I could praise
(In any mean*) thy worth, strike envy dumb;   *way
But I die here, thou liv'st in time to come.
States have their period, statues lost with rust:
Souls to Elysium,[19] Nature yields to dust;
All monuments of arms and power decay,
But that which lives to an eternal day,
Letters preserve; nay, gods with mortal men
Do sympathize by virtue of the pen.
And so shalt thou, sweet Willie. Then proceed,
And in eternal merit fame[20] thy reed.
PAN to thy fleecèd numbers give increase,
And Pales[21] to thy love-thoughts give true peace.
Let fair Feronia (goddess of the woods)[22]
Preserve thy young plants, multiply thy buds.
And whiles thy rams do tup,[23] thy ewes do twin,
Do thou in peaceful shade (from men's rude din)
Add pinions to thy fame, whose active wit
With Hermes'[24] wingèd cap doth suit most fit.

Christopher Brooke.

---

such men to power under James I played a part in much criticism of the reign.

[19] *Elysium*] in Greek mythology, western isles to which the favoured dead departed; in Latin mythology part of the underworld.

[20] *fame*] spread abroad, report.

[21] *Pales*] Roman god of sheep and shepherds.

[22] *Feronia*] cf. Vergil *Aeneid* 7.800, and Horace, Satire 1.5.24.

[23] *tup*] copulate with ewes.

[24] *Hermes*] messenger of the gods, and inventor of the lyre.

Shepherd's Pipe, Eclogue 9

Introduction

This eclogue by Wither is similar to the fifth eclogue in its subject matter: it consists largely of one shepherd-poet encouraging another to write and publish poetry. As noted in the introduction to that work such themes have played a large part in the pastoral tradition. Thirsis argues that there is a virtue and brilliance in Alexis that deserves to be publicly shared in verse. In response Alexis brings forward the usual objections to such an undertaking: insufficient skill, the threat of Envy, and the burden of other work. In the end Alexis agrees that he will undertake public poetry, if a theme presents itself.

Clearly, Thirsis represents Wither, and when this eclogue was reprinted in *Shepherd's Hunting* as Eclogue 5, the name was changed to Roget to make it consistent with the usual pastoral identity of Wither. Alexis is more difficult to identify: in *Shepherd's Hunting* it is dedicated "To Master W.F. of the Middle Temple", and this has led most scholars to identify him with William Ferrar, brother of Nicholas Ferrar.[1] This identification has been extended to the Alexis in *Shepherd's Hunting* III, and the one whose death is lamented in *Britannia's Pastorals*, II, 242ff. However, William Ferrar was still alive after the publication of *Britannia's Pastorals* Book II, and this would throw into the doubt the identity of Alexis in *Shepherd's Pipe* and *Shepherd's Hunting*.[2] Sir William Alexander had presented himself as Alexis in the sonnet sequence, *Aurora* (1604), but the Alexis in this eclogue would not seem to have published poetry. From the

---

[1] Other members of the Middle Temple in these years with the initials W.F. were William Fleetewood, William Freke, and William Fulford.

[2] See J. Doelman, "An Unnoted Funeral Epitaph by Nicholas Ferrar". *Notes and Queries.* December 1992.

beginning of the eclogue it seems clear that Alexis is of higher social stature than Wither.

As it stands in *Shepherd's Pipe*, the eclogue was clearly written after the publication of *Abuses*, but before Wither's imprisonment. In the version in *Shepherd's Hunting* Wither adds a section where he describes himself in prison, thus making it consistent with the setting of the rest of the eclogues in that work.

Thirsis[3] AND
Alexis.[4]

Thirsis.[5]

Alexis, if thy worth do not disdain
The humble friendship of a meaner swain;
Or some more needful business of the day
Urge thee to be too hasty on thy way;
Come (gentle shepherd) rest thee here by me
Under the shadow of this broad-leaved tree.
For though I seem a stranger, yet mine eye
Observes in thee the marks of courtesy;
And if my judgement err not, noted too,
More than in those that more would seem to do:
Such virtues thy rude modesty doth hide
Which by thy[6] proper lustre I espied;
And though long masked in silence they have been,
I have a wisdom through that silence seen.
Yea, I have learnèd knowledge from thy tongue,
And heard when thou hast in concealment sung;
Which me the bolder and more willing made
Thus to invite thee to this homely shade.
And though (it may be) thou couldst never spy

---

3 *Thirsis*] a common pastoral name. A poem entitled "Thirsis' praise of his Mistress", appears in *England's Helicon* (1614); Goodwin includes it in his *Poems of William Browne*.

4 *Alexis*] The name "Alexis" appears in Virgil's Second Eclogue, where he is a young boy; a long tradition going back to at least Servius has connected him with Octavian, that is, the young Caesar Augustus.

5 The following argument appears in the reprinted version of this eclogue in *Shepherd's Hunting*:

> Roget here Alexis moves,
> To embrace the Muses loves;
> 'Bids him never careful seem,
> Of another's disesteem,
> Since to them it may suffice,
> That themselves can justly prize.

6 *thy*] *SH*, Eclogue 5 has "their".

Such worth in me to make me[7] known thereby,
In thee I do; for here my neighbouring sheep
Upon the border of these downs I keep:
Where often thou at pastorals[8] and plays
Hast graced our wakes on summer Holy-days;
And many a time with thee at this cold spring
Met I, to hear your learnèd shepherds sing,
Saw them disporting in the shady groves,
And in chaste sonnets woo their chaster loves:
When I, endued with the meanest skill,
'Mongst others have been urged to tune my quill,
Where (cause but little cunning I had got)
Perhaps thou sawst me, though thou knew'st me not.

    Alexis.

Yes Thirsis, I do know thee and thy name,
Nor is my knowledge grounded all on fame;
Art not thou he, that but this other year,
Scared'st all the wolves and foxes in the sheer?·   ·shire
And in a match at football lately tried
(Having scarce twenty Satyres on thy side)[9]
Held'st play, and though assailed, keptst thy stand
Gainst all the best-tried ruffians in the land?
Didst thou not then in doleful sonnets moan,
When the belovèd of great Pan was gone;[10]
And at the wedding of fair Thame and Rhine,
Sing of their glories to thy Valentine?[11]
I know it, and I must confess that long
In one thing I did do thy nature wrong:
For, till I marked the aim thy Satyres had
I thought them overbold and Thirsis mad,
But since I did more nearly on thee look
I soon perceived that I had all mistook;

---

7 *to make me*] *SH*, ecl. 5 has "I might be".

8 *pastorals*] pastoral games.

9 The original spelling "satyres" has been maintained as it suggests both satires and "satyrs". The reference is to the twenty sections of Wither's *Abuses Stript and Whipt* (1613).

10 *the belovèd of great Pan*] Prince Henry, at whose death Wither wrote and published *Prince Henries Obsequies*.

11 The marriage of Princess Elizabeth to Count Frederick of the Palatine, which took place on Feb. 14, 1613. In celebration Wither published *Epithalamia* (1613).

I saw that of a cynic thou madst show,
Where since I find that thou wert nothing so,
And that of many thou much blame hadst got:
When as thy innocence deserved it not.
But this too good opinion thou hast seemed
To have of me (not so to be esteemed)
Prevails not aught to stay him who doth fear
He rather should reproofs then praises hear:
'Tis true I found thee plain and honest too,
Which made me like, then love, as now I do;
And Thirsis, though a stranger, this I say:
Where I do love I am not coy to stay.

Thirsis.

Thanks gentle swain that dost so soon unfold
What I to thee as gladly would have told,
And thus thy wonted courtesy expressed
In kindly entertaining this request:
Sure I should injury[12] my own content
Or wrong thy love to stand on compliment,
Who hast acquaintance in one word begun
As well as I could in an age have done;
Or by an overweening slowness mar
What thy more wisdom hath brought on so far.
Then sit thou down and I'll my mind declare
As freely, as if we familiars were;
And if thou wilt but deign to give me ear,
Something thou maist for thy more profit hear.

Alexis.

Willingly Thirsis I thy wish obey.

Thirsis.

Then know Alexis from that very day
When as I saw thee at that shepherd's cote
Where each I think of other took first note,
I mean that pastor who by Tavy's springs[13]
Chaste shepherds' loves in sweetest numbers sings,
And in his music (to his greatest fame)

---

12 *injury*] used here as a verb.
13 William Browne.

Hath late made proud the fairest nymphs of Thame;
E'en then methought I did espy in thee
Some unperceived and hidden worth to be,
Which in thy more apparent virtues shined
And among many I in thought divined;
By something my conceit had understood
That thou wert marked one of the Muses' brood.
That made me love thee: and that love I bear
Begat a pity, and that pity care:
Pity I had to see good parts concealed,
Care I had how to have that good revealed,
Since 'tis a fault admitteth no excuse
To possess much and yet put nought in use.
Hereon I vowed (if we two ever met)
The first request what I would strive to get
Should be but this: that thou wouldst shew* thy skill,   *show
How thou couldst tune thy verses to thy quill;
And teach thy Muse in some well-framèd song,
To shew the art thou hast suppressed so long;
Which, if my new[14] acquaintance may obtain,
Thirsis will ever honour this day's gain.

Alexis.

Alas, my small experience scarce can tell
So much as where those nymphs the Muses dwell,
Nor (though my slow conceit still travels on)
Shall I e'er reach to drink of Helicon;
Or if I might so favoured be to taste
What those sweet streams but overflow in waste,
And touch Parnassus where it low'st doth lie,
I fear my skill would hardly flag[15] so high.

Thirsis.

Despair not man: the gods have prized nought
So dear that may not be with labour bought,
Nor need thy pain be great since Fate and Heaven
They (as a blessing) at thy birth have given.

---

14 *new*] provided by *SH,* Eclogue 5; *Shepherd's Pipe* has "my my acquaintance".
15 *flag*] fly unsteadily.

Alexis.

Why say they had?

Thirsis.

Then use their gifts thou must,
Or be ungrateful, and so be unjust;
For if it cannot truly be denied,
Ingratitude men's benefits do hide,
Then more ungrateful must he be by odds[16]
Who doth conceal the bounty of the gods.

Alexis.

That's true indeed, but Envy hateth[17] those
Who seeking fame their hidden skill disclose:
Where else they might (obscured) from her espying
Escape the blasts and danger of envying:
Critics will censure our best strains of wit,
And purblind Ignorance misconstrue it.
All which is bad: yet worse than this doth follow,
Most hate the Muses, and contemn Apollo.

Thirsis.

So let them: why should we their hate esteem?
Is't not enough we of ourselves can deem?*   *judge
'Tis more to their disgrace that we scorn them,
Than unto us that they our art contemn.
Can we have better pastime than to see
Our gross heads may so much deceivèd be,
As to allow those doings best, where wholly
We scoff them to their face, and flout their folly;
Or to behold black Envy in her prime
Die self-consumed, whilst we vie lives with time:
And in despite of her, more fame attain
Than all her malice can wipe out again?

Alexis.

Yea, but if I applied me to those strains,
Who should drive forth my flocks unto the plains,

---

16 *by odds*] by advantage, by his superior position.
17 *hateth*] *SH*, Eclogue 5 has "haunteth".

Which whilst the Muses rest, and leisure crave,
Must watering, folding and attendance have?
For if I leave with wonted care to cherish
Those tender herds: both I and they should perish.

Thirsis.

Alexis, now I see thou dost mistake:
There is no meaning thou thy charge forsake,
Nor would I wish thee so thy self abuse
As to neglect thy calling for thy Muse:
But let these two so of each other borrow,
That they may season mirth, and lessen sorrow.
Thy flock will help thy charges to defray,
Thy Muse to pass the long and tedious day.
Or whilst thou tun'st sweet measures to thy Reed
Thy sheep to listen will more near thee feed,
The wolves will shun them, birds above thee sing,
And lambkins˙ dance about thee in a ring;   ˙small lambs
Nay, which is more: in this thy low estate
Thou in contentment shalt with Monarchs mate:˙   ˙rival
For mighty Pan[18] and Ceres[19] to us grants
Our fields and flocks shall help our outward wants.
The Muses teach us songs to put off cares,
Graced with as rare and sweet conceits as theirs:
And we can think our lasses on the greens
As fair, or fairer then the fairest queens;
Or what is more than most of them shall do,
We'll make their juster fames last longer too,
Having our lines by greatest princes graced
When both their name and memory's defaced.
Therefore, Alexis, though that some disdain
The heavenly music of the rural plain,
What is't to us, if they (o'erseen)[20] contemn
The dainties which were ne'er ordained for them?
And though that there be other some envy
The praises due to sacred poesy,
Let them disdain and fret till they are weary,

---

[18] *Pan*] Greek god of sheep and shepherds, frequently presented as the chief god of pastoral poetry.

[19] *Ceres*] Roman goddess of fertility and crops, frequently associated with the Greek goddess Demeter.

[20] *o'erseen*] deceived, mistaken.

We in ourselves have that shall make us merry:
Which he that wants, and had the power to know it,
Would give his life that he might die a poet.[21]

Alexis.

Thou hast so well (young Thirsis) played thy part
I am almost in love with that sweet art:
And if some power will but inspire my song,
Alexis will not be obscured long.

Thirsis.

Enough kind pastor: but oh, yonder see
Two shepherds, walking on the lay-bank[22] be,[23]
Cuttie and Willie, that so dearly love,
Who are repairing unto yonder grove.
Let's follow them: for never braver swains
Made music to their flocks upon these plains.
They are more worthy, and can better tell
What rare contents do with a poet dwell.
Then whiles our sheep the short sweet grass do shear,
And till the long shade of the hills appear,
We'll hear them sing: for though the one be young,
Never was any that more sweetly sung.

Geo. Wither.

---

[21] See appendix at the end of this eclogue.

[22] *lay-bank*] bank of the lake. "Lay" was an archaic word for a lake or pool.

[23] In *SH*, Eclogue 5 this line reads, "Two honest shepherds walking hither be".

Appendix

In the *Shepherd's Hunting* version of this eclogue the following exchange is added at the end of Thirsis/Roget's second-last speech:

Alexis

A brave persuasion.

Roget

Here thou seest me pent
Within the jaws of strict imprisonment;
A forlorn shepherd, void of all the means,
Whereon man's common hope in danger leans:
Weak in myself. Exposed to the hate
Of those whose Envies are insatiate:
Shut from my friends, banished from all delights,
Nay worse: excluded from the sacred Rites.
Here I do live ('mongst outlaws marked for death)
As one unfit to draw the common breath;
Where those who to be good did never know
Are barred from the means should make them so.
I suffer, cause I wished my country well,
And what I more must bear I cannot tell.
I'm sure they give my body little scope,
And would allow my mind a little hope;
I waste my means, which of itself is slender,
Consume my time (perhaps my fortunes hinder)
And many crosses have, which those that can
Conceive no wrong that hurts another man
Will not take note of, though if half so much
Should light on them, or their own person touch,
Some that themselves (I fear) most worthy think
With all their helps would into baseness shrink;
But spite of hate, and all that spite can do,
I can be patient yet, and merry too;
That slender Muse of mine, by which my name,
Though scarce deserved hath gained a little fame,
Hath made me unto such a Fortune borne,
That all misfortunes I know how to scorn;
Yea, midst these bands can sleight the great'st that be
As much as their disdain misteems of me.
This cave whose very presence some affrights
I have oft made to echo forth delights,

And hope to turn, if any justice be,
Both shame and care on those that wished it me:
For while the world rank villanies affords,
I will not spare to paint them out in words;
Because I thus into these troubles run,
I knew what man could act, e're I begun:
And I'll fulfill what my Muse draws me to,
Maugre all jails, and purgatories too.
For whilst she sets me honest tasks about,
Virtue or she I know will bear me out:
And if by Fate th'abused power of some,
Must in the world's eye leave me overcome,
They shall find one fort yet so fenced I trow,*   *trust
It cannot feel a mortal's overthrow.
This hope and trust that great power did infuse,
That first inspired into my breast a Muse,
By whom I do, and ever will contemn
All these ill haps, my foes' despite, and them.

Shepherd's Pipe, Eclogue 10

Introduction

Like Eclogues 5 and 8, this eclogue concerns the writing of poetry and the inadequate public response to it. Wernocke, who represents Davies, encourages Willie to continue the poetic task begun in his *Britannia's Pastorals*, but Willie responds by lamenting the lack of patronage. His lament, especially in its harking back to the days of Maecenas, recalls that of Cuddie in "October" of *The Shepheardes Calender.* For Willie, both the laurel crown associated with poetry of national significance and the garland associated with regional May-festivals seem to be out of reach.

Wernocke encourages Willie to pursue poetry for the sake of virtue and the life beyond, but at the same time suggests that Willie can address contemporary concerns and morals by guilefully covering them in other dress. He seems to be suggesting that Browne take up a satiric position in opposition to "the world". Willie claims that family pressures prevent him from taking such a role, and so declines Wernocke's advice.

The first book of *Britannia's Pastorals* had provoked some controversy, possibly because of its praise of Essex and Ralegh, and the implicit suggestion that James' reign was unheroic in contrast to that preceding it. However, in spite of what seems to be Willie's rejection of Davies' encouragement of satire here, his second book, published in 1616 was far more satiric and politically dangerous. There he quite directly criticizes the state of the British navy, and promises further satire in the future.

Willie's thoughts in this eclogue may merely be Davies' projection, or they could be an accurate picture of Browne's uncertainty about the satiric mode in the period between the first and second books of *Britannia's Pastorals.*

The language in the eclogue presents many problems. While at times it includes genuine west-country dialect, at others Davies is using archaisms or pseudo-archaisms. The influence of Spenser's diction, particularly that of *The Shepheardes Calender*, is frequently evident.

An Eclogue between young
Willie the singer of his na-
tive Pastorals, and old
Wernocke[1] his friend.

Wernocke.

Willie, why lig'st* thou (man) so woe-be-gone?　　　　*liest
What, been thy rather[2] lambkins[3] ill apaid?[4]
Or, that some dreary chance thy pipe misdone?
Or, hast thou any sheep-cure misassayed?[5]
Or, is some conteck[6] 'twixt thy love and thee?
Or, else some love-work arsy-versy[7] tane?[8]
Or, fates less frolic[9] than they wont to be?
What gars[10] my Willie that he so doth wane?
If it be for thou hast mis-said, or done,
Take keep[11] of thine own counsel; and thou art
As sheen[12] and clear fro* both-twain[13] as the sun:　　　*from
For all swains laud thine haviour,[14] and thine art.

---

[1] A figure named *Wrenock* is mentioned in the December Eclogue of *Shepheardes Calender*, where he is described as "a good olde shephearde" who made Colin Clout "by arte more cunning in the same" (41–2). Renwick and Richard E. McLane have both suggested that in that poem he represents Richard Mulcaster (c. 1530–1611), Spenser's schoolmaster at Merchant Taylors' School. Davies was significantly older than Browne, who attended Oxford while Davies was a writing master at Magdalen College.

[2] *rather*] born earlier in the year. Cf. *SC*, February, 83, "The rather Lambes bene starved with cold.

[3] *lambkins*] little lambs.

[4] *ill apaid*] dissatisfied.

[5] *misassayed*] attempted without success.

[6] *conteck*] strife or debate at law.

[7] *arsy-versy*] upside-down, in confusion.

[8] *tane*] obsolete form of "taken", common in Scotland and north of England at the time.

[9] *frolic*] (adj) joyous or active.

[10] *gars*] originally meaning "to do" or "to cause", pastoral poets such as Davies came to use it to mean "to ail", probably in imitation of Spenser.

[11] *Take keep*] take notice.

[12] *sheen*] beautiful, bright.

[13] "both-twain" would seem to refer to "missaying" and "misdoing."

Mayhap* thine heart (that unneath[15] brook[16] neglect,   *perhaps
And jealous of thy fresh fame) ligs* upon   *lies
Thy rural songs, which rarest[17] clarks* affect,[18]   *clergy
Dreading the descant that mote[19] fall thereon.[20]
Droop not for that (man) but unpleat thy brows,
And blithely, so, fold Envy's up in pleats:
For, fro* thy makings[21] milk and mellie[22] flows   *from
To feed the songster-swains with art's soot-meats.[23]

Willie.

Now, sicker* (Wernocke) thou hast split the mark,   *certainly
Albe[24] that I ne wot[25] I han* mis-sung: *have
But, for I am so young, I dread my wark*   *work
Will be misvalued both of old and young.

Wernocke.

Is thilke* the cause that thou been lig so laid,[26]   *this
Who whilom* no encheason[27] could fore-hail;[28]   *formerly
And caitiff-courage[29] ne'er made mis-apaid,[30]
But with chief youngsters songsters bear'st thy sail?[31]
As swoot[32] as swans thy strains make Thames to ring

---

[14] *haviour*] bearing, manner.

[15] *unneath*] scarcely.

[16] *brook*] endure, bear.

[17] *rarest*] most distinguished, finest.

[18] *affect*] attack. Possibly an allusion to attacks on *Britannia's Pastorals* by churchmen.

[19] *mote*] must or may.

[20] cf. *SP*, Eclogue 1, where Roget complains of those who "descant on my quill".

[21] *makings*] poetry.

[22] *mellie*] honey, from the word "mell".

[23] *soot-meats*] sweetmeats.

[24] *Albe*] although.

[25] *ne wot*] know not.

[26] *laid*] beaten down, brought low.

[27] *encheason*] occasion, cause.

[28] *fore-hail*] greet in advance.

[29] *caitiff-courage*] courage of a wretch or villain.

[30] *mis-apaid*] dissatisfied, discontented. The *OED* cites this as the only instance of the word and describes it as pseudo-archaic. Cf. "ill apaid", line 2.

[31] *bear'st thy sail*] to sail in a particular direction.

Fro* Cotswold where her source her course doth take,   *from
To her wide mouth which vents thy caroling
Beyond the heather and the further lake.
Then up (sad swain) pull fro thy veilèd cheek
Her prop, thy palm: and let thy virelays,[33]
Kill envious cunning swains (whom all do seek)
With envy, at thine earnèd gaudy praise.
Up hither lad, thou reck'st[34] much of thy swink,[35]
When swink ne sweat[36] thou shouldst ne reck[37] for fame;
At Aganippe[38] then, lay thee down to drink
Until thy stomach swell, to raise thy name.
What though time yet han not bedowled[39] thy chin?[40]
Thy dam's dear womb was Helicon to thee;
Where (like a loach[41]) thou drew'st thilke* liquor in,   *this
Which on thy heart-strings ran with music's glee.
Then up betimes, and make the sullen swains
With thy shrill reed such jolly-jouissance,[42]
That they (entranced[43]) may wonder at thy strains;
So, leave of thee ne'er-ending sovenance.[44]

Willie.

Ah, Wernocke, Wernocke, so my sp'rits been steept
In dullness, through these duller times' missawes[45]
Of sick-like music (rhyming rudely cleept),

---

32 *swoot*] sweet.

33 *virelays*] short lyric songs, usually concerning love.

34 *reck'st*] think much of.

35 *swink*] labour, toil.

36 *swink ne sweat*] in medieval English these terms were frequently paired together in this way.

37 *reck*] heed, concern oneself.

38 *Aganippe*] a spring on Mount Helicon, the home of the Muses.

39 *bedowled*] covered with feathers or hair.

40 Throughout the early writings of both Wither and Browne there is repeated reference to their youth.

41 *loach*] a small fish.

42 *jouissance*] Fr., joy, enjoyment. Spenser uses the word in the May eclogue of *Shepheardes Calender*. "To see those folkes make such iouysaunce,/Made my heart after the pype to daunce."

43 *entranced*] thrown into a trance.

44 *sovenance*] remembrance.

45 *missawes*] slanders.

That yer⸱ I pipe well, must be better cause.   ⸱before
Ah, who (with lavish draught, of Aganippe)
Can swill their soul to frolic; so, their Muse,
When courts and camps, that erst the muse did clip,[46]
Do now forlore[47] her; nay, her most abuse?
Now, with their witless, causeless surquedry⸱   ⸱arrogance
They been transposed fro what of yore they were,
That swains, who but to looser luxury
Can shew the way, are now most cherished there.
These times been crimeful (ah) and being so,
Bold swains (deft songsters) sing them criminal;
So, make themselves oft gleeful in their woe:
For thy[48] tho⸱ songsters are misweened[49] of all.   ⸱those
Maecenas[50] wont[51] in blunket[52] liveries
Yclad[53] sike⸱ chanters;[54] but these miser times   ⸱such
Uncase hem⸱ quite, that all may hem despise,   ⸱them
As they don[55] all their best embellished rhymes.
And harvest-queens, of yore, would chaplets make
To crown their scalps that couth⸱ most swootly[56] sing,   ⸱could
And give hem many a gaud[57] at ale[58] or wake,[59]
But now ne reck they of[60] foot carolling.[61]

---

[46] *clip*] embrace.

[47] *forlore*] leave, abandon.

[48] *for thy*] therefore.

[49] *misweened*] misjudged.

[50] *Maecenas*] Gaius Maecenas (d. 8 B.C.), counsellor of the Roman Emperor Augustus, and patron of Horace and Virgil. In the Renaissance he was frequently held up as a model of patronage, and the lack of such patrons bemoaned. See for example the October eclogue in *Shepheardes Calender*, "But ah *Mecoenas* is yclad in claye,/And great *Augustus* long ygoe is dead;" (61–2).

[51] *wont*] was accustomed to.

[52] *blunket*] greyish-blue. Cf. *Shepheardes Calender*, May, 5.

[53] *Yclad*] clothed.

[54] *chanters*] singers.

[55] *don*] past participle of do.

[56] *swootly*] sweetly.

[57] *gaud*] ornament.

[58] *ale*] festival.

[59] Cf. the description of the "Nimph that hight Desart" in *Shepherd's Pipe*, eclogue 11, p. 142.

[60] *ne reck they of*] they do not care for.

[61] *foot carolling*] ? singing on foot.

Enaunter[62] they should be as seem they would,
Or songen loudly for so dear dessert;
Or else be paregal[63] to nymphs of old,
From which their beastlihead[64] now freely start.[65]
Then must they latch[66] the blows of Fates too fell[67]
With their too feeble clutches as they con:*   *can
Or, none regards or guards hem* for their spell,   *them
Tho* they, on point-device,[68] empt[69] Helicon!   *then
There nis[70] thilke* chevisance[71] they whilom had   *this
For piping swoot; sith, with an Hay-de-guise,[72]
Piped by Tom-piper,[73] or a Lorel-lad,[74]
(So be he claws[75] hem) they idolatrize.
And those that should press* proper songs for sale,   *print
Been, in their dooms,[76] so dull; in skill, so crude;
That they had liefer* printen Jacke a vale,[77]   *rather
Or Clym o'Clough[78] (alack) they been so rude!

---

62 *Enaunter*] lest.

63 *paregal*] fully equal.

64 *beastlihead*] beastliness. Cf. *Shepheardes Calender,* May, "Sicke, sicke, alas, and little lack of dead,/But I be relieved by your beastlyhead." (265–6). The gloss to *Shepheardes Calender* defines "beastlihead" as "agreeing to the person of a beast."

65 *start*] escape.

66 *latch*] seize.

67 *fell*] fierce.

68 *on point-device*] perfectly.

69 *empt*] drain.

70 *nis*] is not.

71 *chevisance*] provision. Cf. Spenser (*FQ,* II, ix, 8 and III, xi, 24) who uses the word to mean "chivalric enterprise", based on a false etymology. In *Shepheardes Calender,* May, 92, it seems to be used in the more conventional sense.

72 *Hay-de-guise*] a country dance.

73 *Tom-piper*] "Tom Piper" is referred to in *Shepheardes Calender,* October, 78, where he represents uncouth rural music or poetry makers; according to E.K. he appeals to those "rude wits, whych make more account of a ryming ryband, then of skill grounded upon learning and judgment".

74 *Lorel-lad*] rascal, rogue.

75 *claws*] prob. in this case meaning "flatters" or "cajoles".

76 *dooms*] judgements, opinions.

77 *Jacke a vale*] ?A reference to one of a number of outlaw or rebel figures named Jack, such as Jack Cade or Jack Straw.

78 *Clym o'Clough*] Clym of the Clough, a noted outlaw of northern England,

And sith so few feat[79] songsters in an age
Been founden; few do weigh hem as they been,
For, swains, that con* no skill of holy-rage,[80]   *know
Been foe-men to fair skill's enlaureled Queen.
Enough is me, for thy,[81] that I may vent
My wit's spells to myself, or unto thee
(Dear Wernocke) which dost feel like miscontent
Sith thou, and all unheeded, singed with me.

Wernocke.

Virtue, it's said (and is an old said-saw[82])
Is for herself, to be foresought[83] alone:[84]
Then eftsoons from their case thy shrill pipes draw
And make the welkin[85] ringen with their tone.
Of world, ne* worldy[86] men take thou no keep,   *nor
What the one doth, or what the other say;
For should I so, I so, should Eyne* out-weep;   *eyes
Then, with me; Willie, aye sing "care-away".[87]
It's wood[88] to be sore-pined with wasteful cark[89]
In many a noyful* stour[90] of willing bale[91]   *annoying
For vading[92] toys: but trim wits' poorest wark*   *work

---

famous in ballads and mentioned. He is described in Jonson's *Alchemist* as
"cheating" (I, ii, 45).

79 *feat*] suitable, dextrous.

80 *holy-rage*] the divine fury that set upon prophets. It was sometimes closely
related to poetic fury, especially in the influential *Les Semaines* by the French
poet du Bartas.

81 *for thy*] therefore.

82 *said-saw*] proverb, adage.

83 *foresought*] sought beforehand.

84 This would seem to be a variant on the proverb "Virtue is its own reward"
(Tilley V81).

85 *welkin*] heavens.

86 *worldy*] variant of "worldly"; the original has "worly", which may be
possible as a Scottish variant of the same word.

87 *care-away*] an exclamation of merriment.

88 *wood*] mad, insane.

89 *cark*] burden, care.

90 *stour*] strife, turmoil.

91 *bale*] evil, suffering.

92 *vading*] fading, disappearing.

The upper heav'n han˙ hent[93] fro nether dale.   ˙has
Thilk's[94] all our share of all the quelling[95] heap
Of this world's good: enough is us to tell
How rude the rest been, caduke,[96] and how cheap;
But, laud for well-done works, done all excell![97]
For thy[98] we shoulden take keep of our race
That here we rennen,[99] and what here we doon˙   ˙do
That when we wenden till˙ an other place,   ˙to
Our sovenance may here, ay-gayly[100] wonne.
For, time will undersong[101] us; and our voice
Woll˙ waxen weak; and, our devising lame;   ˙will
For, life is brief; and skills been long, and choice:[102]
Then, spend we Time, that Time may spare our Fame,
Look how breme˙ winter chamfers[103] earth's bleak face;   ˙fierce
So, courbèd[104] eld[105] accoys[106] youth's surquedry;˙   ˙arrogance
And, in the front, deep furrows doon˙ enchase,[107]   ˙does
Enveloped with falling snow a-high.˙   ˙on high
Then nought can be achieved with witty shews,˙   ˙shows
Sith grief of eld accloyen[108] wimble[109] wit;

---

93 *hent*] seized, lifted up.

94 *Thilk's*] this is.

95 *quelling*] abating. Cf. Spenser, *SC,* March, 8.

96 *caduke*] fleeting, liable to fall.

97 *done all excell*] that do surpass all.

98 *for thy*] therefore.

99 *rennen*] obs. form of "run".

100 *ay-gayly*] always gayly.

101 *undersong*] used as a noun meaning "burden" or undermelody in Spenser, Drayton, and Browne; *OED* gives no use as verb. It could be used here to mean that time will reduce them to be merely an "undersong".

102 The proverbial phrase, best-known in its Latin rendering, "Ars longa, vita brevis" originated with Hippocrates in his *Aphorisms.* Chaucer echoed it in *The Parliament of Fowls,* "The lyf so short, the craft so long to lerne,/ Th'assay so hard, so sharpe the conquerynge."

103 *chamfers*] furrows.

104 *courbèd*] bent, crooked.

105 *eld*] old age.

106 *accoys*] calms, appeases.

107 *enchase*] engrave, adorn.

108 *accloyen*] overburden, lame. Cf. *Shepheardes Calender,* Feb., 135, where E.K. glosses it as "encombreth".

109 *wimble*] active. Cf. *Shepheardes Calender,* March, 91 where it is glossed

Then, us behoven, yer⋅ eld sick accrues,[110]   ⋅before
Time to forelay,[111] with spells retarding it.
I not⋅ what blisses is whelmed[112] with heav'n's cope[113]   ⋅know not
So be the pleasance[114] of the Muse be none:
For, when thilk⋅ gleesome joys han hallowed scope[115]   ⋅these
They been as those that heav'n's-folk[116] warble on.
I con⋅ my good; for, now my scalp is frost   ⋅know
Yielding to snow; the crow-feet near mine eyne⋅   ⋅eyes
Been marks of mickle⋅ press[117] I have, that most   ⋅much
Of all glees else allow, han sudden fine.⋅   ⋅end
O how it gars⋅ old Wernocke swink[118] with glee   ⋅causes
In that emprise that chiven⋅ featest[119] fame,   ⋅gains
It heats my heart above ability
To leave perduring[120] sovenance[121] of my name.
And when mine engine[122] han heaved high my thought,
An that on point-device[123] eftsoons[124] yfell,⋅   ⋅fallen
O! how my heart's joy-rapt, as I had caught,
A Princedom to my share, of thilk⋅ newel.[125]   ⋅this
They been of pleasances⋅ the alderbest:[126]   ⋅joys
Then, God to forne,[127] I woll[128] no mo[129] but tho:⋅   ⋅those

---

"quicke".
  [110] *accrues*] grows, increases.
  [111] *forelay*] waylay, hinder.
  [112] *whelmed*] covered, engulfed.
  [113] *cope*] canopy, vault.
  [114] *pleasance*] delight, joy.
  [115] *scope*] subject or theme of writing.
  [116] *heav'ns-folk*] angels.
  [117] *press*] urgency.
  [118] *swink*] trouble, toil.
  [119] *featest*] most suitable, proper.
  [120] *perduring*] lasting, enduring.
  [121] *sovenance*] remembrance.
  [122] *engine*] brain.
  [123] *point-device*] ? perfectly.
  [124] *eftsoons*] soon afterwards, occasionally.
  [125] *newel*] news, novelty. Cf. *Shepheardes Calender*, May, 276.
  [126] *alderbest*] best of all. It is somewhat reminiscent of the German, "aller-beste", meaning "very best".
  [127] *God to forne*] before God.
  [128] *woll*] will.
  [129] *mo*] more.

Tho been the sum of all I loven best:
And for him love I live, else nold[130] I so.
Drive on thy flock then, to the motley plains
Where by some prill,[131] that 'mong the pebbles plods;
Thou, with thine oaten reed, and quaintest strains,
Maist rapt the senior swains, and minor Gods:
That as on Ida,[132] that much-famed Mount,
A shepherd swain that sung less soot* than thou: *sweet
By light love's Goddess,[133] had the grace to mount
To owe* the sheenest[134] Queen that earth did owe;[135]   *possess
So, thou maist, with thy past'ral minstrelsy
Beating the air, atween* resounding hills,   *between
Draw to thee bonibells[136] as smirk,[137] as high,
And wrap hem in thy love begrey* their wills: *against
For (ah) had Phoebus' clarks* the means of some   *clergy
Worse clerks (paraunter)[138] so to sing at ease;
They soon would make high long-winged haggards[139] come;
And vail* unto their lures: so, on hem self.   *submit
For, bright nymphs buxom breasts do eas'ly ope
To let in thirling[140] notes of noted lays:
For, deftly sung they han a charming scope;*   *subject
So, nymphs themselves adore brows girt with bays.
Then, Willie (ah for pity of thine heart
That drooping yearns, at misses of these times)
Take thou thy pipe, and of glee[141] take thy part;
Or cheer thyself with cordials of thy rimes.
Before the world's stern face, the world back-bite

---

130 *nold*] would not.

131 *prill*] a small stream, rill. A west country and Welsh marches word, the two earliest uses of it in *OED* are from Davies.

132 *Ida*] mountain(s) in Phrygia, where Paris was brought up by shepherds.

133 *light love's Goddess*] Venus.

134 *sheenest*] brightest, most beautiful.

135 With the help of Aphrodite, whom Paris had judged the most beautiful goddess, he carried off Helen of Troy.

136 *bonibells*] fair maids. Cf. *Shepheardes Calender*, August, 62.

137 *smirk*] neat, pleasant.

138 *paraunter*] peradventure, by chance.

139 *haggards*] wild female hawks, wild women.

140 *thirling*] penetrating, piercing.

141 *glee*] music. Later in sixteenth century glee came to specifically refer to a three-voice english song without accompaniment.

So slyly that her parts ne'it perceive:[142]
Moral˙ thy matter so, that, though thou smite,   ˙moralize
Thou maist with tickling her dull sense, deceive.[143]
Then hie thee, Willie, to the neighbour wasts˙   ˙wastes
Where thou (as in another world alone)
Maist (while thy flock do feed) blow bitter blasts
On thy loudst pipe, to make ills[144] pertly˙ known.   ˙plainly
For, sith the rude-crude world doon us misplease
That well deserven, tell we her her own;
And let her ken our cunning can, with ease,
Aye shend,˙ or lend her sempitern[145] renown.   ˙disgrace

Willie.

Ah Wernocke, so thy saws mine heart doon thrill
With love of Muses' skill in special,
That I ne wot,[146] on mould[147] what feater[148] skill
Can be yhugged in lording's[149] pectoral.˙   ˙heart
Ne would I it let-be for all the store
In th'uncouth scope of both-twain hemispheres;
Enough is me, *perdie*,˙ nor strive for more   ˙by God
But to be rich in hery[150] for my lears.˙   ˙studies
Ne˙ would I sharen that soul-gladding glee   ˙nor
In th'ever gaudy gardens of the blest;
Not there to han the Muses' company,
Which, God tofore,˙ is of the best, the best.   ˙before
Now, Wernocke, shalt thou see (so mote˙ I thee)   ˙may
That I nill[151] usen any skill so mytch˙   ˙much
(Fair fall my swink)˙ as this so nice, and free,   ˙labour
In case I may my name to heaven stitch.
For why? I am by kind so inly pulled
To these delices;˙ that when I betake   ˙delights
Myself to other lore I more am dulled;

---

[142] *ne'it perceive*] do not perceive it.
[143] Wernocke seems to be advising a subtle, moral poetry.
[144] *ills*] il's (1614).
[145] *sempitern*] eternal.
[146] *ne wot*] do not know.
[147] *on mould*] in the world.
[148] *feater*] more suitable.
[149] *lording's*] little lord's.
[150] *hery*] ? Grosart suggests "praise".
[151] *nill*] will not.

And therefro,* keenly set, I fall to make.   *therefore
But, well-away,[152] thy nis* the way to thriven;   *is not
And, my near kith,[153] for that woll* sore me shend: *will
Who little reck how I by kind am given;
But her would force to swink for thriftier[154] end.
Henceforward then I must assay, and con[155]
My lear[156] in leefull[157] lore, to pleasen them
That, sib[158] to me, would my promotion,
And cark* for that to prank[159] our common stem.   *care
For, now (as wends* the world) no skill to that   *goes
(Or rather but that) thrives; sith swains are now
So full of conteck,[160] that they wot ne[161] what
They would; so, if they could they all would owe.
So fares it in calm seasons with cursed men;
If frennes[162] forbear, at home, hem to invade,
They wry[163] their peace to noy* each other then   *annoy
By pleas,[164] till they decease, or fall, or fade.
So times been keener* now with common swains   *harsher
Than when as foreign foe-men with hem fought:
For, now they swink, but for sly Law-men's gains
Or seld* they should possessen what they ought.   *seldom
But, what for this? To me it little longs
To gab[165] of sikliche[166] notes of misery;
Enough is me to chant swoot* my songs,   *sweetly
And blend hem with my rural minstrelsy.
But, o (my Wernocke) how am I to thee
Obligen, for thy keen re-encouragements

---

152 *well-away*] exclamation of lamentation.
153 *kith*] close friends and family.
154 *thriftier*] more successful, more fortunate.
155 *con*] study, learn, know.
156 *lear*] instruction, learning.
157 *leefull*] lawfull, permissable.
158 *sib*] closely related.
159 *prank*] proudly display. Cf. Spenser, *FQ*, I.iv.14.8; II.ii.36.8; II.iii.6.4.
160 *conteck*] strife, discord.
161 *wot ne*] know not.
162 *frennes*] foreigners, enemies.
163 *wry*] pervert.
164 *pleas*] legal suits.
165 *gab*] speak mockingly of.
166 *sikliche*] sickly, or suchlike. The pun is likely intentional.

To skill so mickle[*] loved and sought of me   [*]much
As this of making with art's elements?
I not[167] how I shall thrive therein; ne[*] how   [*]nor
I shall be dempt[*] of in these nicer[168] times: [*]deemed
But howsoe'er so thou my works allow,
I nill[*] be ill-apaiden[169] with my rimes.   [*]will not

Wernocke.

Thou needst not, Willie; wretch were I to laud
Thee in thy misses: for, I so should be
To th'adulteries of thy wits-scapes,[170] but a baud,
Ne as a friend, in sentence, should be free.
Than, wend thou fairly on, with thine emprise;[171]
Sing clearly, Will, on mine encouragement,
And other swains, more able to devise;
And, fix thee for it, in the firmament.
Enough is me so I may bear a part
Aye in the Muses' choir with those and thee;
I'll sing (at ease) aloud, with cheerful heart,
No base ne meane[172] but tenor[173] of best glee.

Willie.

And I, with thee, woll[*] chant each counter-verse   [*]will
So shrilly that we'll make thilk[*] choir to ring   [*]this
As ever do the angels; who rehearse
The loudest lauds of heav'n's-Lord when they sing.
So, farewell, Wernocke, mickle[*] thanks to thee   [*]much
For thy freedom, that canst so well devise:
Phoebus now goes to glade;[174] then now go we,
Unto our sheds to rest us till he rise.

---

167 *not*] know not.

168 *nicer*] more wanton, more dainty.

169 *ill-apaiden*] poorly rewarded.

170 *wits-scapes*] witty transgressions. A "scape" was often a sexual transgression; it could also mean simply an error, such as a slip of the tongue or pen, or a breaking of wind.

171 *emprise*] enterprise.

172 *meane*] originally the middle part in three-part polyphony, in late sixteenth and seventeenth century it came to refer to the countertenor.

173 In the Renaissance the tenor part usually had the melody in polyphonic music.

174 *glade*] a clear spot in the woods or sky.

Wernocke.

Agreed dear Willie, gent and debonair,
We'll hence, for rheumatic now fares the air.

JO. Davies

To his better beloved than
known friend, M[r]. BROWNE.[175]

Such is the fate of some (write) nowadays
Thinking to win and wear, they break the bays,
As a slow footman[176] striving near to come
A swifter that before him far doth run,
Puffed with the hope of honour's goal to win
Runs out of breath yet furthest off from him.
So do our most of Poets whose Muse flies
About for honour: catch poor butterflies.
But thou, fair friend, not ranked shall be 'mongst those
That makes a mountain where a mole-hill grows;
Thou whose sweet singing pen such lays hath writ
That in an old way, teacheth us now wit;
Thou that wert born and bred to be the man
To turn Apollo's glory into Pan,
And when thou lists of shepherds leave to write,
To great Apollo add again his light;
For never yet, like shepherds forth have come
Whose pipes so sweetly play as thine have done.
Fair Muse of Browne, whose beauty is as pure
As women, Browne that fair and long'st endure:
Still mayst thou as thou dost a lover move,
And as thou dost each mover may thee love,
Whilst I myself, in love with thee must fall,
Browne's Muse the fair Browne woman still will call.

JOHN ONLEY.
Int. Temp.[177]

---

175 The placement of this commendatory poem suggests that Davies' eclogue was originally meant to be the last in the volume, and that the eclogue by Wither which follows was a last-minute addition.

176 *footman*] pedestrian.

177 *Int. Temp.*] Inner Temple. Nothing more is known about Onley.

Shepherd's Pipe, Eclogue 11

Introduction

Shepherd's Pipe begins with Willie encouraging Roget, it ends with the two shepherd/poets taking the opposite roles. Here Roget encourages Willie to continue his Pastorals, despite the threats of critics, and his concerns that he may be too young for such ambitious work. Like the eclogues by Davies and Brooke, it suggests that the whole of Browne's contribution to *Shepherd's Pipe* is an interlude taken by Browne while he considers whether to continue with *Britannia's Pastorals.* The first book of *Britannia's Pastorals* seems relatively innocuous; however, in looking back nostalgically to Essex (V,i,261ff) and Elizabeth (I,ii,322ff), Browne was implicitly criticizing the unheroic nature of James and his advisors. With *Shepherd's Pipe* Browne is adopting the safer course of singing to his friends, as he claims he will now do only, and also the rallying of support from those friends for further work on *Britannia's Pastorals.* More so than the other encouragers, Roget invokes the obligation of the poet to sing publicly, regardless of the consequences, a position consistent with Wither's poetic career in general. The eclogue ends without Willie responding clearly to Roget's arguments, or giving an indication of his plans for *Britannia's Pastorals.* The eclogue provides Wither with an opportunity to express his view of the lofty nature of poetry, and the poetic ambitions he will attempt to fulfill when released from prison.

This eclogue became eclogue four in *Shepherd's Hunting,* and, in that it is set in Roget's prison cell, this eclogue is more akin to the three that first appeared in *Shepherd's Hunting.* This, along with its position in *Shepherd's Pipe,* would suggest that it was written after the other eclogues in that volume. The reference to the May-games makes May the likely month for its composition. This May festival might either be a reference to an actual country festival of competitions of which poetry formed a part, or a veiled allusion to urban poetic competition centred at the Inns of Court. In spite of its setting, little of the eclogue is devoted to describing Wither's situation, a subject he reserved for *Shepherd's Hunting*.

ANOTHER
ECLOGUE:
BY
M^r. George Wither.

Dedicated to his truly loving and worthy friend, M^r
W.BROWNE.

LONDON,

Printed for George Norton.

1614.

TO HIS TRULY BELOVED
loving friend Mr WILLIAM
BROWNE of the Inner
Temple.

Roget.   Willie.

Prithee, Willie: tell me this,
What new thing late happened is,
Thou (that wert the blithest lad)
Art become so wondrous sad,
And so careless of thy quill,
As if thou hadst had no skill.
Thou wert wont to charm thy flocks,
And among these rudest rocks
Hast so cheered me with thy song,
That I have forgot my wrong.
Something hath thee surely crossed,
That thy old wont thou hast lost,
But what is't? Have I aught said
That hath made thee misapaid?[1]
Hath some churl done thee a spite?[2]

---

[1] *misapaid*] discontented.

[2] *spite*] insult, injury.

Dost thou miss a lamb tonight?
Frowns thy fairest shepherds' lass?
Or how comes this ill to pass?
Is there any discontent
Worse than this my banishment?[3]

Willie.

Why, doth that so evil seem,
That thou nothing worse dost deem?·   ·judge
Shepherd, there full many be,
That would change contents· with thee;   ·pleasures
Those that choose their walks at will,
On the valley or the hill.
Or those pleasures boast of can
Groves or fields may yield to man:
Never come to know the rest
Wherewithal thy mind is blest.
Many a one that oft resorts
To make up the troop at sport,
And in company some while
Happens to strain forth a smile,
Feels more want, more outward smart
And more inward grief of heart,
Than this place can bring to thee,
While thy mind remaineth free.
Thou condemn'st my want of mirth,
But what find'st thou in this earth,
Wherein aught may be believed,
Worth to make me joyed, or grieved?
And yet feel I (naitheless)[4]
Part of both I must confess:
Sometime I of mirth do borrow,
Other while as much of sorrow,
But my present state is such,
I'm not joyed nor grieved much.[5]

_____

[3] Wither's imprisonment.

[4] *naitheless*] nonetheless.

[5] The final four lines of this speech are provided from the version in
Shepherd's Hunting. *Shepherd's Pipe* has:

> Seld, yet for such causes small:

> But I grieve not now at all.

It seems that some lines were left out, and when Wither included the eclogue in

Roget.

Why hath Willie then so long,
Now forborne his wonted song?
Wherefore doth he now let fall,
His well-tuned Pastoral?[6]
And my cares that music bar,
Which I more long after far
Than the liberty I want.

Willie.

That were very much to grant,
But doth this hold alway lad,
Those that sing not must be sad?
Didst thou ever that bird hear
Sing well, that sings all the year?
Tom the Piper[7] doth not play
Till he wears his pipe away:
There's a time to slack the string,
And a time to leave to sing.

Roget.

Yea, but no man now is still,
That can sing, or tune a quill.
Now to chant it, were but reason,
Song and music are in season.
Now in this sweet jolly tide,
Is the earth in all her pride.
The fair Lady of the May[8]
Trimmed up in her best array
Hath invited all the swains,
With the lasses of the plains,
To attend upon her sport
At the places of resort.
Coridon[9] (with his bold rout)

Shepherd's Hunting he provided four entirely new lines.

6 *Pastoral*] *Britannia's Pastorals.*

7 *Tom the Piper*] cf. Eclogue 10.

8 *Lady of the May*] cf. *Britannia's Pastorals*, II.iv. 269.

9 *Coridon*] a common pastoral name, appearing in Theocritus' fourth Idyll, and Virgil's second eclogue. A figure named Coridon also plays a major role in *Faerie Queene*, VI.ix. Greg, in *Pastoral Poetry and Pastoral Drama*, p. 115,

Hath already been about
For the elder shepherds' dole:[10]
And fetched in the Summer-Pole;[11]
Whilst the rest have built a bower,
To defend them from a shower,
Sealed so close with boughs all green,
Titan[12] cannot pry between.
Now the dairy wenches dream
Of their strawberries and cream.
And each doth her self advance
To be taken in, to dance.
Every one that knows to sing,
Fits him now for carolling:
So do those tha' hope for meed,*   *reward
Either by the pipe or reed;
And though I am kept away,
I do hear (this very day)
Many learnèd grooms do wend,
For the garlands to contend
Which a nymph that hight Desart,*   *desert
(Long a stranger in this part)
With her own fair hands hath wrought;
A rare work (they say) past thought,
As appeareth by the name,
For she calls them *Wreaths of Fame*.[13]
She hath set in their due place
Every flower that may grace,
And among a thousand moe,*   *more
(Whereof some but serve for show)
She hath wove in Daphne's tree,[14]
That they may not blasted be.

---

identifies the Coridon mentioned in Henry Chettle's *Englandes Mourning Garment* (1603) with Michael Drayton, and it is possible he is the poet intended here.

   [10] *dole*] reward, portion.

   [11] *Summer-Pole*] a flower-decked pole used during summer games or festivals, similar to a Maypole.

   [12] *Titan*] the sun.

   [13] *Wreaths of Fame*] cf. *Britannia's Pastorals*, II.iv.243.

   [14] *Daphne's tree*] Daphne was a Greek nymph, turned into a laurel tree while fleeing from Apollo.

Which with thyme[15] she edged about,
That it might not shatter out.
And that they might wither never,
Intermixed it with Live-ever.[16]
These are to be shared among
Those that do excel for song,
Or their passions can rehearse
In the smooth'st and sweetest verse.
Then for those amid the rest,
That can play and pipe the best,
There's a kidling with the dam,
A fat wether,[17] and a lamb.
And for those that leapen far,
Wrestle, run, and throw the bar,[18]
There's appointed guerdons* too: *rewards
He that best the first can do
Shall for his reward be paid,
With a sheep-hook, fair inlaid
With fine bone, of a strange beast,
That men bring from out the west.
For the next, a scrip[19] of red,
Tasseled with fine coloured thread.
Then for him that's quick'st of foot,
A cup of a maple-root:[20]
Whereupon the skillful man
Hath engraved the loves of Pan.
And the last hath for his due,
A fine napkin wrought with blue.
Then my Willie what moves thee,
Thus forgetful now to be?
What mak'st thou here with a wight
That is shut up from delight,
In a solitary den
As not fit to live with men.

---

15 *thyme*] spelled "time" in the 1614 edition, there may be a pun intended here.

16 *Live-ever*] the plant orpine, also known as "livelong"; so-called because even after being cut it will remain green for a long time.

17 *wether*] a ram.

18 *throw the bar*] a game involving throwing a bar of iron or wood.

19 *scrip*] shepherd's satchel.

20 *Shepherd's Hunting* has "Cups of turned *Maple-root*".

Go my Willie, get thee gone,
Leave me in exile alone.
Hie thee to that merry throng,
And amaze them with thy song.
Thou art young, yet such a lay
Never graced the month of May,
As (if they provoke thy skill)
Thou canst fit unto thy quill.
I with wonder heard thee sing,
At our last year's revelling.[21]
Then I with the rest was free,
When unknown I noted thee:
And perceived the ruder swains,
Envy thy far sweeter strains.
Yea, I saw the lasses cling
Round about thee in a ring:
As if each one jealous were,
Any but herself should hear.
And I know they yet do long
For the res'due of thy song.
Haste thee then to sing it forth,
Take the benefit of worth.
And Desert will sure bequeath
Fame's fair garland for thy wreath.
Hie thee Willie, hie away.

Willie.

Roget, rather let me stay,
And be desolate with thee,
Than at those their revels be.
Nought such is my skill I wis,   *know
As indeed thou deem'st it is.
But whate'er it be, I must
Be content, and shall I trust.
For a song I do not pass,
'Mongst my friends, but what (alas)
Should I have to do with them
That my music do contemn?
Some there are, as well I wot,   *know
That the same yet favour not:

---

[21] Presumably a reference to *Britannia's Pastorals*, Book I. The address to the reader in that work is dated June 18, 1613.

Yet I cannot well avow,
They my carols disallow.
But such malice I have spid,*   *spied
'Tis as bad as if they did.

Roget.

Willie, what may those men be,
Are so ill to malice thee?

Willie.

Some are worthy-well esteemed,
Some without worth are so deemed.
Others of so base a spirit,
They have not esteem, nor merit.

Roget.

What's the wrong?

Willie.

A slight offence,
Wherewithal I can dispense;
But hereafter for their sake,
To myself I'll music make.

Roget.

What, because some clown offends,
Wilt thou punish all thy friends?

Willie.

Honest Roget understand me,
Those that love me may command me.
But thou know'st I am but young,
And the Pastoral I sung,
Is by some supposed to be
(By a strain) too high for me.
So they kindly let me gain,
Not my labour, for my pain.
Trust me, I do wonder why
They should me my own deny.
Though I'm young, I scorn to flit
On the wings of borrowed wit.
I'll make my own feathers rear me,

Whither others cannot bear me.
Yet I'll keep my skill in store,
Till I've seen some winters more.

Roget.

But in earnest mean'st thou so?
Then thou art not wise, I trow.˙   ˙believes
Better shall advise thee Pan,
For thou dost not rightly then:
That's the ready way to blot
All the credit thou hast got.
Rather in thy age's prime,
Get another start of time:
And make those that so fond be,
(Spite of their own dullness) see
That the sacred Muses can
Make a child in years, a man.
It is known what thou canst do,
For it is not long ago,
When that Cuddie, thou, and I
Each the others skill to try,
At Saint Dunstan's charmèd well,[22]
(As some present there can tell)
Sang upon a sudden theme,
Sitting by the crimson stream.
Where, if thou didst well or no,
Yet remains the song to show.
Much experience more I've had,
Of thy skill (thou happy lad)
And would make the world to know it,
But that time will further show it.
Envy makes their tongues now run,
More than doubt of what is done.
For that needs must be thy own,
Or to be some others known:
But how then wilt suit unto
What thou shalt hereafter do?
Or I wonder where is he,
Would with that song part to thee:
Nay, were there so mad a swain,

---

[22] Grundy, p. 84, identifies this as the Devil and St. Dunstan's Tavern in Fleet
St., scene of Ben Jonson's Apollo meetings.

Could such glory sell for gain;
Phoebus would not have combined
That gift with so base a mind.
Never did the Nine[23] impart
The sweet secrets of their art
Unto any that did scorn
To have their fair badge seen worn.
Therefore, unto those that say,
Were they pleased to sing a lay,
They could do't, and will not though;
This I speak, for this I know:
None e'er drunk the Thespian Spring,[24]
And knew how, but he did sing.
For that one infused in man,
Makes him shew't, do what he can;   *show it
Nay those that do only sip,
Or but ev'n their fingers dip,
In that sacred Fount (poor Elves)
Of that brood will shew themselves.   *show
Yea, in hope to get them fame,
They will speak though to their shame;
Let those then at thee repine,
That by their wits measure thine.
Needs those songs must be thy own,
And that one day will be known,
The same imputation too,
I myself do undergo:
But it will be known ere long,
I'm abused, and thou hast wrong,
Who at twice ten hast song more
Than some will do at fourscore.
Cheer thee (honest Willie) then,
And begin thy song again.

Willie.

Fain I would, but I do fear
When again my lines they hear,
If they yield they are my rhymes,   *admit
They will find some other crimes.
And 'tis not safe vent'ring by,

---

23 *the Nine*] the Muses.
24 *Thespian spring*] pertaining to the dramatic or tragic.

Where we see Detraction lie.
For do what I can, I doubt,
She will pick some quarrel out,
And I oft have heard defended,
Little said, and soon amended.

Roget.

Seest thou not in clearest days
Oft thick fogs cloud heaven's rays?
And the vapours that do breathe
From the earth's gross womb beneath,
Seem they not with their black steams,
To pollute the sun's bright beams,
And yet vanish into air,
Leaving them (unblemished) fair?
So (my Willie) shall it be
With Detraction's breath and thee.
It shall never rise so high,
As to stain thy poesy.
Like the sun she oft exhales
Vapours from the rott'nest vales;
But so much her power can do,
That she may dissolve them too.
If thy verse do bravely tower,
As she makes wing, she gets power.
But the higher she doth soar,
She's affronted still the more:
Till she to the high'st hath past,
Then she rests with Fame at last.
Let nought therefore thee affright,
But make forward in thy flight:
For if I could match thy rhyme,
To the very stars I'd climb.
There begin again and fly
Till I reached Eternity.
But (alas) my Muse is slow:
For thy pace she flags° too low.   °flies awkwardly
Yea, the more's her hapless fate,
Her long wings were clipped of late,
And poor I, her fortune rueing,
Am myself put up a-mewing.[25]

---

[25] *mewing*] to moult feathers, to change one's aspect. Hawks were put in a

But if I my cage can rid,
I'll fly where I never did.
And though for her sake I'm crossed;
Though my best hopes I have lost,
And knew she would make my trouble,
Ten times more than ten times double,
I would love and keep her too,
Spite of all the world could do.
For though banished from my flocks,
And confined within these rocks,
Here I waste away the light,
And consume the sullen night;
She doth for my comfort stay,
And keeps many cares away.
Though I miss the flowery fields,
With those sweets the spring-tide yields;
Though I may not see those groves,
Where the shepherds chant their loves,
And the lasses more excel,
Than the sweet-voiced Philomel;[26]
Though of all those pleasures past,
Nothing now remains at last,
But Remembrance (poor relief)
That more makes, than mends, my grief:
She's my mind's companion still,
Maugre˙ Envy's evil will;   ˙in spite of
Whence she should be driven too,
Wert't in mortals' power to do.
She doth tell me where to borrow
Comfort in the midst of sorrow;
Makes the desolatest place
To her presence be a grace,
And the blackest discontents
Be her fairest ornaments.
In my former days of bliss,
Her divine thoughts taught me this,
That from everything I saw,
I could some invention draw;

---

cage at "mewing" time; thus, "to mew" also came to mean "to lock up".

26 *Philomel*] the nightingale; in Ovid's *Metamorphoses* the young woman
Philomel is changed into a nightingale after being raped by her brother-in-law
Tereus.

And raise pleasure to her height,
Through the meanest object's sight,
By the murmur of a spring,
Or the least leaves' rustling.
By a daisy whose leaves spread
Shut when Titan goes to bed,
Or a shady bush or tree,
She could more infuse in me,
Than all Nature's beauties can,
In some other wiser man.
By her help I also now,
Make this churlish place allow
Some things, that may sweeten gladness
In the very gall of sadness.
The dull loneness, the black shade,
That these hanging vaults have made;
The strange music of the waves,
Beating on these hollow caves;
This grim den which rocks emboss,
Overgrown with eldest moss;
The rude portals that give light,
More to Terror than Delight;
This my chamber of Neglect,
Walled about with Disrespect;
From all these, and this dull air,
A fit object for Despair,
She hath taught me by her might
To draw comfort and delight.
Therefore, thou best earthly bliss,
I will cherish thee for this.
Poesy, thou sweet'st content*   *pleasure
That e'er Heav'n to mortals lent:
Though they as a trifle leave thee,
Whose dull thoughts cannot conceive thee;
Though thou be to them a scorn
That to nought but earth are born;
Let my life no longer be,
Than I am in love with thee.
Though our wise ones call it madness,
Let me never taste of gladness,
If I love not thy madd'st fits
Above all their greatest wits.
And though some too seeming holy
Do account thy raptures folly,

Thou dost teach me to contemn
What makes knaves and fools of them.
O high power that oft doth carry
Men above,

Willie.

Good Roget, tarry:
I do fear thou wilt be gone
Quite above my reach anon;
The kind flames of Poesy
Have now borne thy thoughts so high,
That they up in heaven be,
And have quite forgotten me.
Call thyself to mind again:
Are these raptures for a swain,
That attends on lowly sheep
And with simple herds doth keep?

Roget.

Thanks my Willie, I had run
Till that time had lodged the sun:
If thou hadst not made me stay;
But thy pardon here I pray.
Loved Apollo's sacred fire[27]
Had raised up my spirits higher
Through the love of Poesy
Than indeed they use to fly.
But as I said, I say still:
If that I had Willie's skill,
Envy nor Detraction's tongue,
Should e'er make me leave my song;
But I'd sing it every day
Till they pined themselves away.
Be thou then advised in this,
Which both just and fitting is:
Finish what thou hast begun,
Or at least still forward run;
Hail and thunder ill he'll bear
That a blast of wind doth fear;
And if words will thus affray* thee,   *frighten
Prithee how will deeds dismay thee?

---

27 The inspiration of Apollo, the god of poetry.

Do not think so rathe[28] a song
Can pass through the vulgar throng
And escape without a touch,
Or that they can hurt it much.
Frosts we see do nip that thing
Which is forward'st in the spring;
Yet at last for all such lets˙   ˙hindrances
Somewhat of the rest it gets;
And I'm sure that so maist thou.
Therefore, my kind Willie now,
Since thy folding time[29] draws on
And I see thou must be gone,
I no more of this will say
Till we meet next holy-day.

George Wither.

Imitatus est Moschi Idyll. & Meleagri Epigram.
Antholog.lib.7.*I.S.* olim inter *Otia Rustica.*[30]

To his Melisa.[31]

Loud did Cytherea cry,
"If you straggling Cupid spy,
And but bring the news to me,
Your reward a kiss shall be;
You shall (if you him restore)
With a kiss, have something more.

Marks enough the boy's known by,
Try colour, flamy eye,
Subtle heart, and sweetened mouth:
Faining still, but failing Truths,

---

[28] *rathe*] early, before the usual time; in this case, early in Willie's career.

[29] *folding time*] the time for returning sheep to the fold.

[30] "This is an imitation of an idyll of Moschius and an epigram of Meleager. Book 7 of *The Anthology* by J.S. [John Stockwood] formerly among the *Rustic Poems*". Moschus was a Greek poet of Syracuse (fl. 150 B.C.) and Meleager was a Greek poet of Syria (fl. 100 B.C.). His poems were included in what was known as *The Greek Anthology*, a collection of short Greek poems, which circulated in the Middle Ages. An edition of this work was published in London by John Stockwood in 1597 under the title *Progymnasma Scholasticum*.

[31] *Melisa*] not identified.

Daring visage, arms but small;
Yet can strike us gods and all.

Body naked, crafty mind;
Wingèd as a bird and blind;
Little bow, but wounding hearts;
Golden both, and leaden darts.
Burning taper; if you find him,
Without pity, look you bind him.
Pity not his tears or smiles:
Both are false, both forgèd guiles.
Fly it, if a kiss he proffer;
Lips enchanting he will offer,
And his quiver, bow, and candle,
But none of them see you handle.

Poisonèd they are, and such,
As myself I dare not touch;
Hurt no sight, yet pierce the eye,
Thence unto the heart they fly.
Warnèd thus, pray, take some pain,
T'help me to my boy again."

Thus, while Cytherea cried him,
Sweet, within thine eyes I spied him.
Thence, he slyly shot at mine,
Struck my heart and crept to thine.
Pay you, sweet, the promised fee,
Him, I'll swear, I did not see.

FINIS.

THE SHEPHERDS

Hunting :

Being,

CERTAINE EGLOGS

written during the time of the
Authors Imprifonment in the
Marfhalfey.

BY
GEORGE VVITHER,
Gentleman.

LONDON:
Printed by THOMAS SNODHAM
for *George Norton*, and are to be fold
at the figne of the red-Bull, neere
Temple-barre. 1615.

THE SHEPHERD'S Hunting:

Being,
CERTAIN ECLOGUES
written during the time of the
author's imprisonment in the
Marshalsea.[1]

BY
GEORGE WITHER,
Gentleman.

LONDON:

Printed by Thomas Snodham[2]
for George Norton,[3] and are to be sold
at the sign of the Red Bull, near
Temple Bar.[4] 1615.

---

[1] The Marshalsea prison was located in Southwark, across the Thames from Westminster. It was frequently used for political prisoners tried at the Court of King's Bench. Political prisoners in Wither's time were liable to be imprisoned in any of a number of different London prisons. At times, the political inmates were purposely kept in different prisons in order to prevent them having contact. Such was the case with those arrested in the Essex rebellion (Christopher Harding et al., *Imprisonment in England and Wales: A Concise History*, (London: Croom Helm, 1985), p. 85).

[2] *Thomas Snodham*] printer in London, ca. 1609–1625.

[3] *George Norton*] bookseller in London, ca. 1610–1624.

[4] Temple Bar was in the west of London, near the Inns of Court.

TO THOSE
HONOURED, NO-
BLE, AND RIGHT
Virtuous Friends, my Visi-
tants in the Marshalsea:[5]

AND,
TO ALL OTHER, MY
UNKNOWN FAVOURITES,
who either privately or publicly wished
me well in my imprisonment.

Noble Friends: you whose virtues made me first in love with Virtue,[6] and whose worths, made me be thought worthy of your loves: I have now at last (you see) by God's assistance and your encouragement, run through the Purgatory of imprisonment, and by the worthy favour of a just Prince, stand free again, without the least touch of dejected baseness.[7] Seeing, therefore, I was grown beyond my Hope so fortunate (after acknowledgement of my Creator's love, together with the unequaled clemency of so gracious a Sovereign), I was troubled to think by what means I might express my thankfulness to so many well-deserving friends. No way I found to my desire, neither yet ability to perform when I found it. But at length considering with myself what you were, that is, such who favour honesty for no second reason but because you yourselves are good; and aim at no other reward but the witness of a sound conscience that you do well, I found that thankfulness would prove the acceptablest present to suit with your dispositions; and that I imagined could be no way better expressed than in manifesting your courtesies, and giving consent to

---

[5] While from this work it would seem that Wither was allowed visitors while in the Marshalsea, in *A Satyre* he claims "That not alone my liberty is barr'd,/But the resort of friends (which is more hard.)" (*Juvenilia*, sig. 2D6r.).

[6] Although it does not play a large part in this poem, Wither's self-presentation as the lover of "Fair Virtue" figures prominently in the volume *Faire-Virtue, the Mistresse of Phil'Aret* (1622).

[7] Wither was released from the Marshalsea on July 26, 1614, approximately four months after he had been imprisoned. See Allan Pritchard, "*Abuses Stript and Whipt* and Wither's Imprisonment", *RES*, new series 14 (1963), p. 22. In *A Satyre* he suggests that James has graced him "with the stile of Honesty" (*Juvenilia*, sig. 2D3r.).

your reasonable demands. For the first, I confess (with thanks to the disposer of all things, and a true grateful heart towards you,) so many were the unexpected visitations and unhoped kindnesses received both from some among you of my acquaintance, and many other unknown well-willers of my cause, that I was persuaded to entertain a much better conceit of the time than I lately conceived; and assured myself that Virtue had far more followers then I supposed.[8]

Somewhat it disturbed me to behold our age's Favourites, whilst they frowned on my honest enterprises, to take unto their protections the egregioust[9] fopperies; yet much more was my contentment, in that I was respected by so many of you, amongst whom there are some, who can and may as much disesteem these, as they neglect me. Nor could I fear their malice or contempt, whilst I enjoyed your favours, who (howsoever you are undervalued by fools for a time) shall leave unto your posterity so noble a memory, that your names shall be reverenced by Kings, when many of these who now flourish with [A5r] a show of usurped greatness, shall either wear out of being, or dispoiled of all their patched reputation, grow contemptible in the eyes of their beloved mistress the world. Your love is that (enabling me with patience to endure what is already past) hath made me (also) careful better to prepare myself for all future misadventures, by bringing to my consideration, what the passion of my just discontentments had almost quite banished from my remembrance.

Further, to declare my thankfulness, in making apparent my willing mind to be commanded in any services of love, which you shall think fit (though I want ability to perform great matters), yet I have according to some of your requests been contented to give way to the printing of these Eclogues, which, though it to many seem a sleight[10] matter, yet being well considered of, may prove a strong argument of my readiness to give you content in a greater matter.[11]

---

8 *Abuses Stript and Whipt* presents a bleak picture of the corruption of the time.

9 *egregioust*] most egregious, shocking.

10 *sleight*] slight, but in this context the noun *sleight*, meaning sheep-pasture, may also be relevant. The first usage cited in *OED* is not until 1670.

11 Frequently throughout his early poems, Wither hints that he will someday write much greater work of a martial nature. For example, in *Prince Henries Obsequies* he hopes that he may write of an anticipated Protestant conquest of Rome. In this context his important poetic work would come:

Then I perhaps, that now tune dolefull layes,

For they being (as you well know) begotten with little care, and preserved with less respect, gave sufficient evidence that I meant (rather than any way to deceive your trust) to give the world occasion of calling my discretion in question, as I now assure myself this will; and the sooner, because such expectations (I perceive) there are, of I know not what inventions, as would have been frustrated though I had employed the utmost and very best of my endeavours.

Notwithstanding, for your sakes, I have here adventured once again to make trial of the world's censures; and what hath received being, from your Loves, I here rededicated to your Worths, which if your noble dispositions will like well of, or if you will but reasonably respect what yourselves drew me unto, I shall be nothing displeased at others' cavils, but resting myself contented with your good opinions, scorn all the rabble of uncharitable detractors; for none I know will malign it except those, who either particularly malice my person, or profess themselves enemies to my former books; who (saving those that were incensed on others' speeches) as divers of you (according to your protestations) have observed, are either open enemies of our Church; men notoriously guilty of some particular abuses therein taxed,[12] such malicious critics who have the repute of being judicious, by detracting from others; or at best such gulls,[13] as never approve anything good, or learned, but either that which their shallow apprehensions can apply to the soothing of their own opinions, or what (indeed rather) they understand not.

Trust me, how illsoever it hath been rewarded, my love to my country is inviolate, my thankfulness to you unfeigned, my endeavour to do every man good, all my aim content with honesty, and this my pains (if it may be so termed) more to avoid idleness, than for affectation

---

Amongst their zealous triumphs may presume

To sing at least some petty Captains praise:

Meanwhile I will some other worke assume. (*Juvenilia*, (1622), p. 370) Similarly, in *A Satyre* he vows to play his oaten pipe, "Untill *Bellona* with her Trumpe awake me" (*Juvenilia*, sig. Ee7v).

[12] In *Abuses Stript and Whipt* Wither claimed that he was not attacking individual figures, but merely vice in general: "thou maist think (perhaps) these *Satyres* sting thee,/Where onely thine owne guiltinesse doth wring thee" (*Juvenilia*, sig. B4v). However, in *A Satyre* he admits that he hoped they would be read in a deep way (*Juvenilia*, sig. Dd4v).

[13] *gulls*] credulous persons, fools.

of praise. And if notwithstanding all this, I must yet, not only rest my self content that my innocency hath escaped with strict imprisonment[14] (to the impairing of my state, and hindrance of my fortunes), but also be constrained to see my guiltless lines, suffer the despite[15] of all tongues; yet for my further encouragement, let me entreat the continuance of your first respect, wherein I shall find that comfort as will be sufficient to make me set light and so much contemn all the malice of my adversaries, that ready to burst with the venom of their own hearts, they shall see

> My mind enamoured on fair Virtue's's[16] light
> Ascends the limits of their bleàrèd sight,
> And placed above their envy, doth contemn,
> Nay, sit and laugh at their disdain and them.

But noble friends, I make question neither of yours, nor any honest man's respect, and therefore will no further urge at, nor trouble your patience: only this I'll say, that you may not think me too well-conceited of myself. Though the time were to blame in ill-requiting my honest endeavours, which in the eyes of the world deserved better, yet somewhat I am assured there was in me worthy that punishment which, when God shall give me grace to see and amend, I doubt not but to find that regard as will be fitting for so much merit as my labours may justly challenge. Meanwhile, the better to hold myself in esteem with you, and amend the world's opinion of Virtue, I will study to amend myself, that I may be yet more worthy to be called

Your Friend,

GEO. WITHER.

---

[14] "Strict imprisonment" refers to what was better known as "close prison", that is, an imprisonment where the prisoner was not allowed to freely roam about the prison, as was usual at the time, but was confined by shackles. Such confinement was more often used with political prisoners than with other types (Harding, p. 82). Cf. *A Satyre, Juvenilia*, sig. Dd6r.

[15] *despite*] injury, malice.

[16] "Fair Virtue" recurs throughout Wither's early poetry as the figure which guides the reader. She is most prominent in the pastoral poem *Faire-Virtue, the Mistresse of Phil'Aret*, written about the time of *Shepherd's Hunting*, but not published until 1622. In parts of that poem she seems to be an allegorical representation of a real woman.

Shepherd's Hunting, Eclogue 1

Introduction

Unlike the two eclogues by Wither that appeared first in *Shepherd's Pipe*, those in *Shepherd's Hunting* largely concern his own situation, that is, his imprisonment from March to July 1614. Much more so than Browne's eclogues in *Shepherd's Pipe*, these first three in *Shepherd's Hunting* form a series: in each Wither provides more information about his imprisonment to a growing circle of friends.

In this eclogue Willie visits Roget imprisoned in his cave, but for the most part Roget comforts and consoles Willie. He invokes the traditional consolation of the liberty of the mind, and declines to dwell on his imprisonment or the reasons for it. Because of this attitude, his cave/prison can be the setting for song. The song which he sings turns the imprisonment into a lesson on avoiding the fetters of sin and Hell. Overall, it is a more sombre song than the lays of love usual on the Plain. Most significantly it takes on a decidedly Christian cast as Wither invokes the traditional association of the shepherd god Pan with Christ, and cites David as the epitome of the shepherd-poet. Overall, we find in this eclogue an indication of the direction Wither would later take in his religious verse.

The first Eclogue.

ARGUMENT.

Willie leaves his flock a while,
Visits Roget in exile;
Where, though prisoned, he doth find,
He's still free that's free in mind;
And in trouble no defence
Is so firm as innocence.

Roget.[1]   *Willie.*[2]

Willie, thou now full jolly tun'st thy reeds,
   Making the Nymphs enamoured on thy strains,
And whilst thy harmless flock unscared feeds,
Hast the contentment, of hills, groves, and plains:
Trust me, I joy thou and thy Muse so speeds
In such an age, where so much mischief reigns;
   And to my care it some redress will be,
   Fortune hath so much grace, to smile on thee.

Willie.

To smile on me? I ne'er yet knew her smile,
Unless 'twere when she purposed to deceive me;
Many a train, and many a painted wile[3]
She casts, in hope of freedom to bereave me:
Yet now, because she sees I scorned her guile
To fawn on fools, she for my Muse doth leave me,
   And here of late, her wonted spite doth tend,
   To work me care, by frowning on my friend.

Roget.

Why then I see her copper-coin's no starling,[4]
'Twill not be current still, for all the guilding;[5]

---

[1] Throughout *Shepherd's Hunting* Roget represents Wither himself. When *Shepherd's Hunting* was reprinted as part of Wither's *Juvenilia* in 1622 the name Roget was changed to Philarete in all eclogues.

[2] As in the eclogues of *Shepheard's Pipe,* Willie represents William Browne.

[3] *wile*] trick, artifice.

A knave, or fool must ever be her darling,
For they have minds to all occasions yielding;
If we get any thing by all our parling[6]
It seems an apple, but it proves a wilding:[7]
  But let that pass; sweet shepherd tell me this,
  For what beloved friend thy sorrow is.

Willie.

Wrong me not Roget: dost thou suffer here,
And ask me for what friend it is I grieve?
Can I suppose thy love to me is dear,
Or this thy joy for my content believe:
When thou think'st thy cares touch not me as near,
Or that I pin thy sorrows at my sleeve?
  Roget, my faith in thee hath had that trust,
  I never thought to find thee so unjust.

Roget.

Why Willie?

Willie.

    Prithee do not ask me why:
Doth it diminish any of thy care,
That I in freedom maken melody,
And think'st I cannot as well somewhat spare
From my delight, to moan thy misery?
'Tis time our loves should these suspects forbear:
  Thou art that friend, which thou unnamed should'st know,
  And not have drawn my love in question so.

Roget.

Forgive me, and I'll pardon thy mistake,
And so shall this thy gentle-anger cease,
(I never of thy love will question make)
Whilst that the number of our days increase;

---

4 *starling*] sterling, in this case meaning genuine money.

5 This would seem to be a proverbial saying; cf. John Lyly *Euphues,* "There
is copper coin of the stamp that gold is, yet is it not current" (ed. Morris William
Croll and Harry Clemon, [New York: Russell and Russell, 1916]), p. 170.

6 *parling*] speaking, negotiating.

7 *wilding*] a wild apple, or crab-apple.

Yet to myself, I much might seem to take,
And something near unto presumption prease:˙   ˙press
    To think me worthy love from such a spirit,
    But that I know thy kindness, past my merit.

Besides, methought thou spak'st now of a friend,
That seemed more grievous discontents to bear;
Some things I find that do in show offend,
Which to my patience little trouble are,
And they ere long I hope will have an end;
Or though they have not, much I do not care.
    So this it was made me that question move,
    And not suspect of honest Willie's love.

Willie.

Alas, thou art exiled from thy flock,
And quite beyond the deserts here confined,
Hast nothing to converse with but a rock,
Or at least outlaws in their caves half pined,[8]
And dost thou at thy own misfortune mock,
Making thyself too to thyself unkind?
    When heretofore we talked we did embrace,
    But now I scarce can come to see thy face.

Roget.

Yet all that, Willie, is not worth thy sorrow,
For I have mirth here thou would'st not believe:
From deepest cares the highest joys I borrow.
If aught chance out this day may make me grieve,
I'll learn to mend, or scorn it by tomorrow;
This barren place yields somewhat to relieve:
    For I have found sufficient to content me,
    And more true bliss, than ever freedom lent me.

Willie.

Are prisons then grown places of delight?

Roget.

'Tis as the conscience of the prisoners:
The very grates are able to affright

---

[8] *pined*] tormented, starved, wasted.

The guilty man, that knows his deeds amiss;
All outward pleasures are exiled quite,
And it is nothing (of itself) but this:
    Abhorred-loneness, darkness, sadness, pains,
    Num'n-cold,[9] sharp-hunger, scorching thirst and chains.

Willie.

And these are nothing?

Roget.

——————————— Nothing yet to me:
Only my friends' restraint is all my pain,
And, since I truly find my conscience free
From that my loneness too I reap some gain.

Willie.

But grant in this no discontentment be,
It doth thy wished liberty restrain,
And to thy soul I think there's nothing nearer,
For I could never hear thee prize aught dearer.

Roget.

True, I did ever set it at a rate
Too dear for any mortal's worth to buy;
'Tis not our greatest shepherd's whole estate
Shall purchase from me my least liberty,
But I am subject to the powers of fate,
And to obey them is no slavery.
    They may do much, but when they have done all,
    Only my body they may bring in thrall.

And 'tis not that (my Willie) 'tis my mind;
My mind's more precious freedom I so weigh.
A thousand ways they may my body bind,
In thousand thralls, but ne'er my mind betray;
And thence it is that I contentment find,
And bear with patience this my load away.
    I'm still myself, and that I'd rather be,
    Than to be Lord of all these downs in fee.[10]

——————————

    [9] *num'n-cold*] numbing cold.

    [10] *in fee*] to hold in absolute and rightful possession.[10]

Willie.

Nobly resolved and I do joy to hear't,
For 'tis the mind of man indeed that's all;
There's nought so hard but a brave heart will bear't,
And guiltless men count great afflictions small;
They'll look on death and torment, yet not fear't,
Because they know 'tis rising so to fall.
        Tyrants may boast they to much power are born,
        Yet he hath more that tyrannies can scorn.

Roget.

'Tis right, but I no tyrannies endure,
Nor have I suffered aught worth name of care.

Willie.

Whate'er thou'lt call't, thou may'st, but I am sure,
Many more pine that much less painèd are;
Thy look methinks doth say thy meaning's pure,
And by this past I find what thou dost dare;
        But I could never yet the reason know,
        Why thou art lodged in this house of woe.

Roget.

Nor I, by Pan, nor never hope to do,
But thus it pleases some; and I do guess
Partly a cause that moves them thereunto,
Which neither will avail me to express,
Nor thee to hear, and therefore let it go.[11]
We must not say, they do so, that oppress;
        Yet I shall ne'er to sooth them or the times,
        Injure my self by bearing others' crimes.

Willie.

Then now thou may'st speak freely, there's none hears,
But he whom I do hope thou dost not doubt.

---

[11] In *A Satyre* Wither comes closer to revealing explicitly the reasons for his imprisonment: he has offended certain Peers who believe that the "Man like Monster" (sig. Dd4v) he depicted in *Abuses Stript and Whipt* represented some particular Lord.

Roget.

True: but if doors and walls have gotten ears,
And closet-whisperings may be spread about,
Do not blame him that in such causes fears
What in his passion he may blunder out:
 In such a place, and such strict times as these,
 Where what we speak is took as others please.

But yet tomorrow if thou come this way,
I'll tell thee all my story to the end;
'Tis long, and now I fear thou canst not stay,
Because thy flock must watered be and penned,
And night begins to muffle up the day;
Which to inform thee how alone I spend,
I'll only sing a sorry prisoner's lay
 I framed this morn, which though it suits not fields,
 Is such as fits me, and sad thralldom yields.

Willie.

Well, I will set my kit[12] another string,
And play unto it whilst that thou dost sing.

SONNET.

Roget.

Now that my body dead-alive,
Bereaved of comfort lies in thrall,
Do thou my soul begin to thrive,
And unto honey, turn this gall;
 So shall we both through outward woe,
 The way to inward comfort know.

For all that food my flesh I give,
Doth keep in me this mortal breath.
So souls on meditations live,
And shun thereby immortal Death;
 Nor art thou ever nearer rest,
 Than when thou find'st me most opprest.

---

[12] A small pocket-sized fiddle with three or four strings. While at the time kits were played by all classes they were especially associated with rustic musicians.

First think my soul: if I have foes
That take a pleasure in my care,
And to procure these outward woes,
Have thus entrapped me unawares;
    Thou should'st by much more careful be,
    Since greater foes lay wait for thee.

Then, when mewed[13] up in grates of steel,
Minding those joys mine eyes do miss,
Thou find'st no torment thou dost feel
So grievous as privation is;
    Muse how the damned in flames that glow,
    Pine in the loss of bliss they know.

Thou seest there's given so great might
To some that are but clay as I,
Their very anger can affright;
Which if in any thou espy,
    Thus think: if mortals' frowns strike fear,
    How dreadful will God's wrath appear?

By my late hopes that now are crost,
Consider those that firmer be;
And make the freedom I have lost,
A means that may remember thee:[14]
    Had Christ not thy Redeemer been,
    What horrid thrall thou hadst been in.

These iron chains, the bolts of steel,
Which other poor offenders grind,
The wants and cares which they do feel
May bring some greater thing to mind:
    For by their grief thou shalt do well
    To think upon the pains of Hell.

Or when through me thou seest a man
Condemned unto a mortal death,
How sad he looks, how pale, how wan,
Drawing with fear his panting breath:
    Think if in that such grief thou see,
    How sad will, Go ye cursèd, be.[15]

---

13 *mewed*] confined, shut up; from the word "mew", the cage in which hawks
were kept. Wither presents himself as a bird singing in a cage in *A Satyre*: "in the
Cage, my old harsh notes I sing" ("To the King's Most Excellent Maiestie").

14 *Remember*] remind.

Again, when he that feared to die
(Past hope) doth see his pardon brought,
Read but the joy that's in his eye,
And then convey it to thy thought.
　　There think, betwixt my heart and thee,
　　How sweet will, Come ye blessèd, be.[16]

Thus if thou do, though closed here,
My bondage I shall deem the less;
I neither shall have cause to fear,
Nor yet bewail my sad distress:
　　For whether live, or pine, or die,
　　We shall have bliss eternally.

Willie.

Trust me, I see the cage doth some birds good,
And if they do not suffer too much wrong,
Will teach them sweeter descants than the wood:
Believe't, I like the subject of thy song.
It shows thou art in no distempered mood;
But cause to hear the residue I long,
　　My sheep tomorrow I will nearer bring,
　　And spend the day to hear thee talk and sing.

Yet ere we part, Roget to me aread,[17]
Of whom thou learnedst to make such songs as these;
I never yet heard any shepherd's reed
Tune in mishap, a strain that more could please.
Surely thou dost invoke at this thy need
Some power, that we neglect in other lays;
　　For here's a name, and words, that but few swains
　　Have mentioned at their meeting on the plains.[18]

---

15 *Go ye cursèd*] from Jesus' description of the Day of Judgement in the Gospel of Matthew: "Then shall he say also unto them on the left hand, Depart from me, ye cursed, into everlasting fire, prepared for the devil and his angels:" (Matt. 25:41).

16 *Come ye blessèd*] also from Jesus' description of the Day of Judgement: "Then shall the King say unto them on his right hand, Come, ye blessed of my Father, inherit the kingdom prepared for you from the foundation of the world." (Matt. 25:34).

17 *aread*] declare, utter.

18 The reference is to the religious note with which Roget ended his song.

Roget.

Indeed 'tis true, and they are sore to blame
They do so much neglect it in their songs;
For, thence proceedeth such a worthy fame,
As is not subject unto Envy's wrongs;
That is the most to-be-respected name
Of our true Pan, whose worth sits on all tongues,[19]
  And the most ancient shepherds use to praise
  In sacred anthems sung on Holy Days.

He that first taught his music such a strain,
Was that sweet shepherd,[20] who (until a King)
Kept sheep upon the honey-milky plain,
That is enriched by Jordan's watering.
He in his troubles eased the body's pains,
By measures raised to the soul's ravishing;[21]
  And his sweet numbers[22] only most divine,
  Gave the first being to this song of mine.

Willie.

Let his good spirit ever with thee dwell,
That I might hear such music every day.

Roget.

Thanks, but would now it pleased thee to play.
Yet sure 'tis late: thy wether[23] rings his bell,
And swains, to fold or homeward drive away.

---

[19] *Pan*] The Greek god of shepherds, he was frequently associated with Christ by medieval and Renaissance allegorists. Cf. the gloss to the April eclogue in *The Shepheardes Calender.* "by Pan is here meant the most famous and victorious King, her highnesse Father, late of worthy memorye K. Henry the eyght. And by that name, oftymes (as hereafter appeareth) be noted kings and mighty Potentates: And in some place Christ himselfe, who is the verye Pan and god of Shepheardes."

[20] *sweet shepherd*] David.

[21] A reference to David playing his harp before Saul (I Sam. 16:14–23).

[22] *His sweet numbers*] the Psalms. In 1619 Wither turned to the task of paraphrasing the Psalms in verse: arising from this work were the publications *A Preparation to the Psalter* (1619), *Exercises upon the First Psalm* (1620), and *The Psalmes of David* (1632).

[23] *wether*] a ram, most often a castrated one, to whose neck was attached a bell to help in leading the flock.

Willie.

And yon goes Cuddie: therefore fare thou well;
I'll make his sheep for me a little stay,
And if thou think it fit I'll bring him too
    Next morning hither.

Roget.

Prithee Willie do.

FINIS.

Shepherd's Hunting, Eclogue 2

Introduction

Willie returns with Cuddie to hear Roget tell his story. As in Eclogues 5 and 8 of *Shepherd's Pipe,* Cuddie likely represents Christopher Brooke. The eclogue begins with reference to the public response to his imprisonment, but then quickly moves on to Roget's recounting of the events leading up to it. The bulk of the eclogue is a description of Wither's *Abuses Stript and Whipt,* the individual sections of that work being described as Roget's "dogs". There is little indication of the particulars that got him into trouble. Roget claims that he is not suited for the pastoral verse he wrote before, and has turned to satire, first in minor ways, and now with an extended work.

Once again the eclogue concludes with a song: this one focuses on the "shepherdess" of Roget, a figure who cannot be identified. That Roget wishes to be "within her arms" would seem to rule out identifying her with Princess Elizabeth, whose patronage is referred to earlier in the eclogue. Once again, the eclogue concludes with a promise that Roget will continue his story at their next visit.

The Second Eclogue.

ARGUMENT.

Cuddie tells how all the swains,
Pity Roget on the plains:
Who requested, doth relate
The true cause of his estate,
Which broke off because 'twas long,
They begin a three-men's song.

Willie. Cuddie. Roget.

Roget, thy old friend Cuddie here and I,
Are come to visit thee in these thy bands,
Whilst both our flocks in an inclosure by
Do pick the thin grass from the fallowed lands.
He tells me thy restraint of liberty
Each one throughout the country understands,
    And there is not a gentle-natur'd lad
    On all these downs, but for thy sake is sad.

Cuddie.

Not thy acquaintance and thy friends alone,
Pity thy close restraint, as friends should do;
But some that have but seen thee, for thee moan;
Yea, many that did never see thee too.
Some deem thee in a fault, and most in none;
So divers ways do divers rumours go:
    And at all meetings where our shepherds be,
    Now the main news that's extant, is of thee.

Roget.

Why, this is somewhat yet: had I but kept
Sheep on the mountains, till the day of doom,
My name should in obscurity have slept,
In brakes, in briars, shrubbèd furze and broom,[1]
Into the world's wide ear it had not crept,
Nor in so many men's thoughts found a room.[2]

---

[1] *broom*] a yellow-flowered shrub.

[2] At no point in his career was Wither concerned with avoiding publicity.

But what cause of my sufferings do they know?
Good Cuddie, tell me how doth rumour go.

Cuddie.

Faith, 'tis uncertain, some speak this, some that;
Some dare say nought, yet seem to think a cause;
And many a one prating he knows not what,
Comes out with proverbs and old ancient saws,
As if he thought thee guiltless, and yet not;
Then doth he speak half sentences, then pause:
    "That what the most would say, we may suppose —
    But what to say the rumour is, none knows."[3]

Roget.

Nor care I greatly, for it skills* not much,   *matters
What the unsteady common people deems:
His conscience doth not always feel least touch,
That blameless in the sight of others seems;
My cause is honest, and because 'tis such,
I hold it so, and not for men's esteems:
    If they speak justly well of me, I'm glad;
    If falsely evil, it ne'er makes me sad.

Willie.

I like that mind, but Roget you are quite
Beside the matter that I long to hear:
Remember what you promised yesternight,
You'd put us off with other talk I fear.
Thou know'st that honest Cuddie's heart's upright,
And none but he, except myself, is near:
    Come, therefore, and betwixt us two relate
    The true occasion of thy present state.

Roget.

My friends, I will: you know I am a swain,
That kept a poor flock here upon this plain,
Who though it seems, I could do nothing less;
Can make a song, and woo a shepherdess.
And not alone the fairest where I live,

---

3 I have taken these two lines to be a representation of the contradictory
speech of the spreader of rumours.

Have heard me sing, and favours deigned to give:
But though I say't, the noblest nymph of Thame,
Hath graced my verse, unto my greater fame.[4]
Yet being young, and not much seeking praise,
I was not noted out for shepherd's lays,
Nor feeding flocks, yea, known as others be:
For the delight that most possessed me
Was hunting foxes, wolves, and beasts of prey
That spoil our folds, and bear our lambs away:[5]
For this, as also for the love I bear
Unto my country, I laid by all care
Of gain, or of preferment, with desire
Only to keep that state I had entire.
And like a true grown huntsman, sought to speed
Myself with hounds of rare and choicest breed,
Whose names and natures ere I further go,
Because you are my friends I'll let you know.
My best esteemèd dog that I did find,
Was by descent of old Acteon's kind;[6]
A brach,[7] which, if I do not aim amiss,
For all the world is just like one of his;
She's named *Love*,[8] and scarce yet knows her duty;
Her dam's my lady's pretty beagle, *Beauty*.
I bred her up myself with wondrous charge,
Until she grew to be exceeding large;
And waxed so wanton that I did abhor it,
And put her out amongst my neighbours for it.
The next is *Lust*, a hound that's kept abroad,
'Mongst some of mine acquaintance, but a toad
Is not more loathsome; 'tis a cur will range
Extremely, and is ever full of mange;
And 'cause it is infectious, she's not wunt[9]

---

[4] The reference is to Princess Elizabeth, whose marriage to Frederick, Elector Palatine, was celebrated by Wither in the poem *Epithalamia* (1613). The marriage was also celebrated by Brooke and Browne in *Two Elegies* (1613).

[5] The reference is to the attacks he made in *Abuses Stript and Whipt*.

[6] In Greek myth Acteon was changed into a stag by the goddess Artemis, and killed by his own hounds.

[7] *brach*] a hound that hunts by scent, usually a female.

[8] *Love*] the title of the first section of *Abuses Stript and Whipt*. From this point, the "hounds" listed are the titles of the sections of *Abuses* in order.

[9] *wunt*] archaic spelling of "wont", at the time "wunt" would have been the

To come among the rest, but when they hunt.
Hate is the third, a hound both deep and long:
His sire is true, or else, supposed wrong.
He'll have a snap at all that pass him by,
And yet pursues his game most eagerly.
With him goes *Envy* coupled, a lean cur;
And she'll hold out, hunt we ne'er so far,
She pineth much, and feedeth little too,
Yet stands and snarleth at the rest that do.
Then there's *Revenge*, a wondrous deep-mouth'd dog,
So fleet, I'm fain to hunt him with a clog;[10]
Yet many times he'll much outstrip his bounds,
And hunts not closely with the other hounds.
He'll venture on a lion in his ire
Cursed *Choler* was his dam, and *Wrong* his sire.
This *Choler* is a brach, that's very old,
And spends her mouth[11] too much to have it hold;
She's very testy, an unpleasing cur,
That bites the very stones, if they but stir;
Or when that aught but her displeasure moves,
She'll bite and snap at any one she loves.
But my quick-scented'st dog is *Jealousy:*
The truest of this breed's in Italy.
The dam of mine would hardly fill a glove,
It was a lady's little dog, called *Love;*
The sire a poor deformed cur named *Fear,*
As shaggèd and as rough as is a bear;
And yet the whelp turned after neither kind:
For he is very large, and near-hand blind.
At the first sight he hath a pretty culler,˙   ˙colour
But doth not seem so when you view him fuller;
A vile suspicious beast, his looks are bad,
And I do fear in time he will grow mad.
To him I couple *Avarice*, still poor,
Yet she devours as much as twenty more;
A thousand horse she in her paunch can put,
Yet whine as if she had an empty gut;
And having gorged what might a land have found,
She'll catch for more, and hide it in the ground.

---

usual pronunciation.
  [10] *clog*] a piece of wood attached to the neck or leg to prevent escape.
  [11] *spends her mouth*] barks on seeing the game.

Ambition is a hound as greedy full,
But her for all the daintiest bits doth cull;*   *select
He scorns to lick up crumbs beneath the table,
He'll fetch't from boards and shelves if he be able;
Nay, he can climb if need be, and for that,
With him I hunt the marten[12] and the cat.[13]
And yet sometimes in mounting he's so quick,
He fetches falls, are like to break his neck.
Fear is well-mouthed, but subject to *Distrust*:
A stranger cannot make him take a crust.
A little thing will soon his courage quail,
And 'twixt his legs he ever claps his tail.
With him *Despair* often coupled goes,
Which by his roaring mouth each huntsman knows.
None hath a better mind unto the gain,*   *prey
But he gives off, and always seemeth lame.
My bloodhound *Cruelty*, as swift as wind,
Hunts to the death, and never comes behind;
Who, but she's strapped and muzzled too withal,
Would eat her fellows, and the prey and all;
And yet she cares not much for any food,
Unless it be the purest harmless blood.
All these are kept abroad at charge of many,
They do not cost me in a year a penny.
But there's two coupling of a middling size,
That seldom pass the sight of my own eyes.
Hope, on whose head I've laid[14] my life to pawn;
Compassion, that on every one will fawn;
This would, when 'twas a whelp, with rabbits play,
Or lambs, and let them go unhurt away;
Nay, now she is of growth, she'll now and then,
Catch you a hare, and let her go again.
The two last, *Joy* and *Sorrow*, 'tis a wonder,
Can ne'er agree, nor ne'er bide far asunder.
Joy's ever wanton, and no order knows:
She'll run at larks, or stand and bark at crows.
Sorrow goes by her, and ne'er moves his eye;

---

[12] While the original has "martin", given the pairing with "cat" it seems more likely that the marten, a fur-bearing mammal, is intended.

[13] There was a species of wild cat (*felis catus*) in England in the early seventeenth century.

[14] from *Juvenilia* (1622). 1615 edition has "led".

Yet both do serve to help make up the cry.
Then comes behind all these to bear the bass,[15]
Two couple more of a larger race;
Such wide-mouth'd trollops, that 'twould do you good
To hear their loud loud[16] echoes tear the wood.
There's *Vanity*, who by his gaudy hide,
May far away from all the rest be spied;
Though huge, yet quick, for he's now here, now there,
Nay, look about you, and he's everywhere;
And ever with the rest, and still in chase.
Right so, *Inconstancy* fills every place,
And yet so strange a fickle-natured hound,
Look for him, and he's nowhere to be found.
Weakness is no fair dog unto the eye,
And yet he hath his proper quality.
But there's *Presumption*: when he heat hath got,
He drowns the thunder, and the cannon-shot;
And when at start he his full roaring makes,
The earth doth tremble, and the heaven shakes.
These were my dogs, ten couple just in all,
Whom by the name of *Satyres* I do call;
Mad curs they be, and I can ne'er come nigh them,
But I'm in danger to be bitten by them.
Much pains I took, and spent days not a few,
To make them keep together, and hunt true;
Which yet I do suppose had never bin,˙   ˙been
But that I had a *Scourge* to keep them in.[17]
Now when that I this kennel first had got,
Out of my own demesnes[18] I hunted not,
Save on these downs, or among yonder rocks,
After those beasts that spoiled our parish flocks;
Nor during that time, was I ever wont,
With all my kennel in one day to hunt.
Nor had done yet, but that this other year,
Some beasts of prey, that haunt the deserts here,
Did not alone for many nights together

---

15 *bear the bass*] to sing or play the bass part of a piece of music.

16 *loud loud*] from *Juvenilia* (1622); 1615 ed. has "loud land".

17 *Abuses Stript and Whipt* concluded with a section entitled "A Scourge".

18 *demesnes*] lands occupied by the owner himself, or less precisely, simply lands. By his "demesnes" Wither is likely referring to his ancestral home near Bentworth, or possibly that area of Hampshire in general.

Devour, sometime a lamb, sometime a wether,[19]
And so disquiet many a poor man's herd,
But that of losing all they were afeared.
Yea, I among the rest did fare as bad,
Or rather worse, for the best ˙Ewes I had,   ˙Hopes.[20]
(Whose breed should be my means of life and gain)
Were in one evening by these monsters slain;
Which mischief I resolved to repay,
Or else grow desp'rate, and hunt all away.
For in a fury (such as you shall see
Huntsmen in missing of their sport will be)
I vowed a monster should not lurk about,
In all this province, but I'd find him out;
And thereupon without respect or care,
How lame, how full, or how unfit they were,
In haste unkenneled all my roaring crew,
Who were as mad as if my mind they knew;
And ere they trailed a flight-shot,[21] the fierce curs
Had roused a hart, and through brakes and furze,
Followed at gaze so close that *Love* and *Fear*
Got in together, so had surely there
Quite overthrown him, but that *Hope* thrust in
'Twixt both, and saved the pinching of his skin;
Whereby he 'scaped, till coursing overthwart,[22]
Despair came in, and gripped him to the heart.
I hallowed[23] in the res'due to the fall,
And for an entrance there I fleshed[24] them all.
Which having done, I dipped my staff in blood,
And onward led my Thunder to the wood;
Where what they did, I'll tell you out anon:
My keeper calls me, and I must be gone.
Go, if you please, a while: attend your flocks;
And when the sun is over yonder rocks,
Come to this cave again where I will be,

---

[19] *wether*] a castrated ram that would lead the flock.

[20] *Hopes*] Wither's marginal note. These hopes may have been for some position at court.

[21] *flight-shot*] the distance an arrow is shot.

[22] *overthwart*] *OED* gives the following meanings: athwart, opposite, here and there, all about.

[23] *hallowed*] to urge on dogs with shouts.

[24] *fleshed*] to reward a dog with some of the flesh of the kill.

If that my guardian so much favour me.
>But ere we part, let each one sing a strain,
>And then go turn your sheep into the plain.

Willie.

I am content.

Cuddie.

As well content am I.

Roget.

Then Will, begin, and we'll the rest supply.

SONG.

Willie.

Shepherd, would these gates were ope,
Thou might'st take with us thy fortune.

Roget.

No, I'll make this narrow scope,
Since my fate doth so importune
>Means unto a wider hope.

Cuddie.

Would thy shepherdess were here,
>Who beloved loves thee so dearly.

Roget.

Not for both your flocks, I swear,
And the gain they yield you yearly,
>Would I so much wrong my dear.

Yet, to me, nor to this place,
Would she now be long a stranger:
She would hold it no disgrace,
(If she feared not more my danger)
>Where I am to shew her face.

Willie.

Shepherd, we would wish no harms,
But something that might content thee.

Roget.

Wish me then within her arms,
And that wish will ne'er repent me,
    If your wishes might prove charms.

Willie.

Be thy prison her embrace,
Be thy air her sweetest breathing.

Cuddie.

Be thy prospect her fair face,
For each look a kiss bequeathing,
    And appoint thyself the place.

Roget.

Nay, pray, hold there, for I should scantly then,
Come meet you here this afternoon again;
But fare you well, since wishes have no power,
Let us depart, and keep the pointed hour.

FINIS.

Shepherd's Hunting, Eclogue 3

Introduction

In this eclogue Roget continues and completes the story of his satires and subsequent imprisonment. Alexis has been added to the circle of listeners.[1] Roget suggests that his satires caught many people, and destroyed reputations, but once again no specifics are given. Although he is imprisoned, his "dogs" continue to roam; this likely is in reference to the popular success of *Abuses Stript and Whipt,* which in addition to the five editions published in 1613, had another issued in 1614. Despite Wither's imprisonment, there is no evidence to suggest that the work itself was suppressed.

This success serves as a consolation to Roget, and both his comforters and Roget himself predict that he and his work will outlive his enemies. In spite of the attractions of the pastoral life that Alexis mentions, Roget is willing to bear his imprisonment, and continue to sing within it. He explains in a song how he accepts his situation in a way that recalls his speeches to Willie in Eclogue 1: his mind is free, and he has the satisfaction of knowing his satires have had and will continue to have the desired effect.

In connecting his satire to the will of God, Wither is very much anticipating his later prophetic stance.

---

[1] On Alexis' identity see the introduction to *Shepherd's Pipe,* Eclogue 9.

The third Eclogue.

ARGUMENT.

Roget set with his three friends,
Here his hunting story ends;
Kind Alexis with much ruth,
Wails the banished shepherd's youth;
But he slighteth Fortune's stings,
And in spite of thraldom sings.

Roget. Cuddie. Alexis. Willie.

So now I see y'are shepherds of your word:
Thus were you wont to promise, and to do.

Cuddie.

More than our promise is we can afford,
We come ourselves, and bring another too:
Alexis whom thou know'st well is no foe,
    Who loves thee much; and I do know that he
    Would fain a hearer of thy hunting be.

Roget.

Alexis you are welcome, for you know
You cannot be but welcome where I am;
You ever were a friend of mine in show,
And I have found you are indeed the same.
Upon my first restraint you hither came,
    And proffered me more tokens of your love,
    Than it were fit my small deserts should prove.

Alexis.

T'is still your use to underprize your merit:
Be not so coy to take my proffered love;
T'will neither unbeseem your worth nor spirit.
To offer court'sy doth thy friend behove;
And which are so, this is a place to prove.
    Then once again I say, if cause there be,
    First make a trial, if thou please, of me.

Roget.

Thanks, good Alexis: sit down by me here;
I have a task, these shepherds know, to do;
A tale already told this morn well near,
With which I very fain would forward go,
And am as willing thou shouldst hear it too;
     But thou canst never understand this last,
     Till I have also told thee what is past.

Willie.

Roget, it shall not need, for I presumed,
Your loves to each were firm, and was so bold,
That so much on myself I have assumed,
To make him know what is already told:
If I have done amiss then you may scold.
     But in my telling I prevised˙ this: ˙foresaw
     He knows not whose, nor to what end it is.

Roget.

Well, now he may, for here my tale goes on:
My eager dogs and I to wood are gone,
Where beating through the coverts[2] every hound
A several game had in a moment found;
I rated˙ them, but they pursued their prey,   ˙scolded
And as it fell (by hap˙) took all one way.   ˙chance
Then I began with quicker speed to follow,
And teased them on with a more cheerful hallow,˙   ˙loud shout
That soon we passed many weary miles,
Tracing the subtle game through all these wiles.
These doubled, they redoubled on the scent,
Still keeping in full chase where'er they went:
Up hills, down cliffs, through bogs, and over plains,
Stretching their muscle to the highest strains
That when some thicket hid them from mine eye,
My ear was ravished with their melody.
Nor crossed we only ditches, hedges, furrows,
But hamlets, tithings,[3] parishes, and boroughs.[4]

---

   2 *coverts*] hiding places.

   3 *tithings*] rural divisions of ten households.

   4 *boroughs*] Snodham, 1615, has "burrows"; the two words were frequently interchanged, and "boroughs" makes more sense in the list of human settlements

They followed wheresoev'r the game did go,
Through kitchen, parlour, hall, and chamber too;
And as they passed the city and the court,
My Prince looked out, and deigned to view my sport;
Which then (although I suffer for it now)
(If some say true) he liking, did allow;
And so much (had I had but wit to stay)
I might myself (perhaps) have heard him say;
But I that time, as much as any daring,
More for my pleasure than my safety caring;
Seeing fresh game from every loop-hole rise,
Crossing by thousands still before their eyes;
After I rushed, and following close my *Hounds*
Some beasts I found lie dead, some full of wounds
Among the willows, scarce with strength to move.
One I found here, another there, whom *Love*
Had gripped to death; and in the selfsame state,
Lay one devoured by *Envy*, one by *Hate*;
Lust had bit some, but I soon passed beside them,
Their festered wounds so stunk, none could abide them.[5]
Choler hurt divers, but *Revenge* killed more;
Fear frighted all, behind him and before.
Despair drove on a huge and mighty heap,
Forcing some down from rocks and hills to leap:
Some into water, some into the fire,
So on themselves he made them wreak his ire;
But I remember as I passed that way,
Where the great King and Prince of Shepherds[6] lay,
About the walls were hid some once more known,
That my fell cur Ambition had o'erthrown.
Many I heard pursued by *Pity* cry,
And oft I saw my bloodhound *Cruelty*,
Eating her passage even to the heart,
Whither once gotten, she is loath to part.
All plied it well, and made so loud a plea,
'Twas heard through *Britain*, and beyond the sea;
Some rated˙ them, some stormed, some liked the game,   ˙scolded

given here.
  [5] For the sake of rhythm, rhyme and sense, I have supplied "them" here. Both
Snodham, 1615, and White, 1615, have only "abide".
  [6] *great King and Prince of Shepherds*] Chaucer and Spenser were both buried
in Westminster Abbey.

Some thought me worthy praise, some worthy blame.
But I not fearing th'one, misteeming[7] t'other,
Both, in shrill hallows[8] and loud yearnings[9] smother:
Yea, the strong-mettled and my long-breathèd[10] crew,
Seeing the game increasing in their view,
Grew the more frolic, and the course's length
Gave better breath, and added to their strength;
Which Jove perceiving, for Jove heard their cries,
Rumbling amongst the spheres' concavities;
He marked their course and courages increase,
Saying, 'twere pity such a chase should cease;
And therewith swore their mouths should never wast,[11]
But hunt as long's* mortality did last.   *long as
Soon did they feel the power of his great gift,
And I began to find their pace more swift;
I followed, and I rated,* but in vain,   *scolded
Strived to o'ertake, or take them up again;
They never stayed since, neither nights nor days,
But to and fro still run a thousand ways.
Yea often to this place where now I lie,
They'll wheel about to cheer me with their cry;
And one day in good time will vengeance take
On some offenders, for their master's sake.
For know, my friends, my freedom in this sort
For them I lose, and making myself sport.

> *Willie.*

Why Roget, was there any harm in this?

> *Roget.*

No Willie, and I hope yet none there is.

> *Willie.*

How comes this then?

---

7 *misteeming*] misesteeming.

8 *hallows*] loud shouts.

9 *yearnings*] eager cries of hounds upon seeing the game.

10 *long-breathèd*] long-winded.

11 *wast*] waste.

Roget.

    Note and I'll tell thee how.
Thou know'st that Truth and Innocency now,
If placed with meanness, suffers more despite   ·scorn
Than villainies, accompanied with might;
But thus it fell, while that my *Hounds* pursued
Their noisome prey, and every field lay strewed
With monsters, hurt and slain 'mongst many a beast;
Some viler, and more subtle than the rest,
On whom the bitch called *Envy*, happed to light;
And as her wont is, did so surely bite,
That though she left behind small outward smarts,
The wounds were deep, and rankled to their hearts.
Then joining to some other that of late
Were very eagerly pursued by *Hate*,
To fit their purpose having taken leisure,
Did thus conspire to work me a displeasure.
For imitation far surpassing apes,
They laid aside their fox, and wolvish shapes,
And shrouded in the skins of harmless sheep,
Into byways, and open-paths did creep;
Where they (as hardly drawing breath) did lie,
Shewing· their wounds to every passerby;   ·showing
To make them think that they were sheep so foiled
And by my dogs in their late hunting spoiled.
Beside some other that envied my game,
And for their pastime kept such Monsters tame —
As you do know there's many for their pleasure,
Keep foxes, bears, and wolves, as some great treasure —
And so did store of these, I speak of, do.
Who seeing that my kennel had affrighted,
Or hurt some vermin wherein they delighted,
And finding their own power by much too weak
Their malice on my innocence to wreak;[12]
Swollen with the deepest rancour of despite,
Some of our greatest shepherds' folds by night
They closely entered; and there having stained
Their hands in villainy, of me they plained,·   ·complained
Affirming, without shame or honesty,
I and my dogs had done it purposely;
Whereat they stormed, and called me to a trial,[13]

---

[12] Wither's attackers.

Where innocence prevails not, nor denial;
But for that cause here in this place I lie,
Where none so merry as my dogs and I.

Cuddie.

Believe it, here's a tale will suiten well,
For shepherds in another age to tell.

Willie.

And Roget shall be thought on with delight,
For this hereafter many a winter's night,
For of this sport another age will ring.
Yea, nymphs unborn now, of the same shall sing,
    When not a beauty on our greens shall play
    That hath not heard of Roget's hunting day.

Roget.

It may be so, for if that gentle swain,
Who wones˚ by Tavy,[14] on the western plain,   ˚dwells
Would make the song, such life his verse can give,
Then I do know my name might ever live.

Alexis.

But tell me: are our plains and nymphs forgot,
And canst thou frolic in thy trouble be?

Roget.

Can I, Alexis, say'st thou? Can I not
That am resolved to scorn more misery?

Alexis.

Oh, but thy youth's yet green, and young blood hot,
And liberty must needs be sweet to thee;
But now most sweet whilst every bushy vale,
And grove and hill rings of the nightingale.
Methinks when thou rememb'rest those sweet lays,
Which thou wouldst lead thy shepherdess to hear

---

13 There is no evidence that there was a formal trial before Wither's imprisonment.

14 *Tavy*] a river in Devon, upon which Tavistock, the birthplace of Browne, is situated.

Each evening forth among the leavy* sprays,   *leafy
The thought of that should make thy freedom dear;
For now whilst every nymph on holy-days
Sports with some jolly lad, and maketh cheer,
  Thine sighs for thee, and mewed up[15] from resort,
  Will neither play herself, nor see their sport.

There's shepherds that were many a morning wont
Unto their boys to leave the tender herd,
And bear thee company when thou didst hunt.
Cannot their songs thou hast so gladly heard,
Nor thy missed pleasure make thee think upon't,
But seems all vain, now that was once endeared.
  It cannot be, for I could make relation,
  How for less cause thou hast been deep in passion.

Roget.

'Tis true: my tender heart was ever yet
Too capable of such conceits as these;
I never saw that object but from it,
The passions of my love, I could increase
Those things which move not other men a whit,[16]
I can, and do make use of, if I please:
  When I am sad, to sadness I apply,
  Each bird, and tree, and flower that I pass by.

So when I will be merry, I as well
Something for mirth from every thing can draw,
From misery, from prisons, nay from Hell,
And as when to my mind, grief gives a flaw,
Best comforts do but make my woes more fell;*   *terrible
So when I'm bent to mirth, from mischief's paw
  (Though ceas'd upon me) I would something cull,[17]
  That spite of care should make my joys more full.

I feel those wants Alexis thou dost name,
Which spite of youth's affections I sustain;
Or else for what is't I have gotten fame,
And am more known than many an elder swain?
If such desires I had not learned to tame,

---

[15] *mewed up*] caged.
[16] *whit*] smallest bit.
[17] *cull*] select.

Since many pipe much better on this plain;
> But tune your reeds, and I will in a song
> Express my care, and how I take this wrong.

SONNET.

I that erstwhile the world's sweet air did draw,
(Graced by the fairest ever mortal saw);
Now closely pent, with walls of ruthless stone,
Consume my days, and nights, and all alone.

When I was wont to sing of shepherds' loves,
My walks were fields, and downs, and hills and groves;
But now (alas) so strict is my hard doom,
Fields, downs, hills, groves, & all's but one poor room.

Each morn as soon as daylight did appear,
With Nature's music birds would charm mine ear;
Which now (instead) of their melodious strains,
Hear rattling shackles, gyves,[18] and bolts, and chains.

But though that all the world's delight forsake me,
I have a Muse and she shall music make;
Whose airy notes in spite of closest cages,
Shall give content to me, and after ages.

Nor do I pass for all this outward ill.
My heart's the same, and undejected still;
And which is more than some in freedom win:
I have true rest, and peace, and joy within.

And then my mind that spite of prison's free,
Whene'er she pleases, anywhere can be;
She's in an hour in France, Rome, Turkey, Spain,
In earth, in hell, in heaven, and here again.

Yet there's another comfort in my woe:
My cause is spread, and all the world doth know
My fault's no more but speaking truth and reason,
Nor debt, nor theft, nor murther,[19] rape, nor treason.

Nor shall my foes with all their might and power,
Wipe out their shame, nor yet this fame of our;
Which when they find they shall my fate envy,

---

[18] *gyves*] leg fetters.
[19] *murther*] murder.

Till they grow lean, and sick, and mad, and die.

Then though my body here in prison rot,
And my poor Satyrs seem a while forgot;
Yet when both fame and life have left those men,
My verse and I'll revive and live again.

So thus enclosed, I bear affliction's load,
But with more true content than some abroad;
For whilst their thoughts do feel my scourge's sting,
In bands I'll leap, and dance, and laugh, and sing.

Alexis.

Why now I see thou droop'st not with thy care,
Neither exclaim'st thou on thy hunting day;
But dost with unchanged resolution bear,
The heavy burthen˙ of exile away,   ˙burden
All that did truly know thee did conceive,
Thy actions with thy spirit still agreed;
Their good conceit thou dost no whit bereave,
But showest that thou art still thyself indeed.
     If that thy mind to baseness now descends,
     Thou'lt injure Virtue, and deceive thy friends.

Willie.

Alexis, he will injure Virtue much,
But more his friends, and most of all himself,
If on that common bar[20] his mind but touch,
It wracks[21] his fame upon disgrace's shelf:
Yet Roget, if thou steer but on the course,
That in thy just adventure is begun,
No thwarting tide, nor adverse blast shall force
Thy bark without the channel's bounds to run.
Thou art the same thou wert for aught I see,
When thou didst freely on the mountains hunt;
In nothing changed yet, unless it be
More merrily disposed than thou wert wont.
Still keep thee thus, so other men shall know,
Virtue can give content in midst of woe.
And he though mightiness with frowns doth threat,
To be yet innocent is to be great.

---

[20] *bar*] sand bank.
[21] *wracks*] destroys, shipwrecks.

Thrive and farewell.

Alexis.

In this thy trouble flourish.

Cuddie.

While those that wish thee ill, fret, pine and perish.

FINIS.

A Postscript
To the READERS.

If you have read this, and received any content,[22] I am glad though it be not so much as I could wish you; if you think it idle, why then I see we are not likely to fall out: for I am just of your minds. Yet weigh it well before you run too far in your censures, lest this prove less barren of wit than you of courtesy. It is very true (I know not by what chance) that I have of late been so highly beholding to Opinion, that I wonder how I crept so much into her favour; and (if I did think it worthy the fearing) I should be afraid that she, having so undeservedly befriended me beyond my hope or expectation, will, upon as little cause, ere long, again pick some quarrel against me; and it may be, means to make use of this, which I know must needs come far short of their expectation, who by their earnest desire of it seemed to be fore-possessed with a far better conceit than I can believe it proves worthy of. So much at least I doubted, and therefore loath to deceive the world (though it often beguile me), I kept it to myself, indeed not dreaming ever to see it published. But now, by the overmuch persuasion of some friends, I have been constrained to expose it to the general view. Which seeing I have done, some things I desire thee to take notice of. First, that I am he who to pleasure my friend, have framed myself a content out of that which would otherwise discontent me. Secondly, that I have coveted more to effect what I think truly honest in itself, than by a seeming show of art, to catch the vain blasts of uncertain Opinion. This that I have here written was no part

---

22 *content*] satisfaction.

of my study,[23] but only a recreation in imprisonment; and a trifle, neither in my conceit fitting, nor by me intended to be made common. Yet some, and it should seem esteeming it worthy more respect than I did, took pains to copy it out unknown to me, and in my absence got it both authorized and prepared for the press; so that if I had not hindered it, last Michaelmas term[24] had been troubled with it. I was much blamed by some friends for withstanding it, to whose request I should more easily have consented, but that I thought (as indeed I yet do) I should thereby more disparage myself, than content them. For I doubt I shall be supposed one of those, who, out of their arrogant desire of a little preposterous Fame, thrust into the world every unseasoned trifle that drops out of their unsettled brains; whose baseness how much I hate, those that know me can witness, for if I were so affected, I might perhaps present the world with as many several poems as I have seen years;[25] and justly make myself appear to be the author of some things that others have shamefully usurped and made use of as their own. But I will be content other men should own some of those issues of the brain, for I would be loath to confess all that might in that kind call me father. Neither shall any more of them, by my consent, in haste again trouble the world, unless I know which way to benefit it with less prejudice to my own estate. And therefore if any of those less serious poems which are already dispersed into my friends' hands come amongst you, let not their publication be imputed to me, nor their lightness be any disparagement to what hath been since more seriously written,[26] seeing it is but such stuff as riper judgements have in their far older years been much more guilty of.

---

[23] Frequently in his poetry from this period, Wither hints that he is planning some serious work. This more serious work may be the hymns and biblical paraphrases that he began to publish in 1619.

[24] *Michaelmas term*] the court sessions beginning shortly after Michaelmas on Sept. 29. *Shepherd's Hunting* had been entered into the Stationer's Register on Oct. 8, 1614.

[25] Some of this early poetry may have appeared in *Fidelia*, a volume of love poetry published in 1615.

[26] These more serious writings could be *Abuses Stript and Whipt* or the hymns and biblical paraphrases referred to above.

I know an indifferent critic may find many faults as well in the sleightness[27] of this present subject, as in the erring from the true nature of an eclogue; moreover, it altogether concerns myself, which divers may dislike. But neither can be done on just cause. The first hath been answered already; the last might consider that I was there where my own estate was chiefly to be looked unto, and all the comfort I could minister unto myself little enough.

If any man deem it worthy his reading, I shall be glad; if he think his pains ill-bestowed, let him blame himself for meddling with that concerned him not. I neither recommended it to him, neither cared whether he read it or no, because I know those that were desirous of it, will esteem the same as much as I expect they should.

But it is not unlikely, some will think I have in divers places been more wanton (as they take it) than befitteth a Satyrist; yet their severity I fear not, because I am assured all that I ever yet did, was free from obscenity. Neither am I so cynical, but that I think a modest expression of such amorous conceits as suit with Reason, will yet very well become my years; in which not to have feeling of the power of love, were as great an argument of much stupidity, as an over-sottish affection were of extreme folly. Lastly, if you think it hath not well answered the title of the *Shepherd's Hunting*, go quarrel with the stationer, who bid himself godfather, and imposed the name according to his own liking; and if you, or he, find any other faults, pray mend them.

   Valete.[28]

   FINIS.

---

[27] *sleightness*] craftiness. "Slightness" might also be intended here. Cf. p. 159, footnote 10.

[28] *valete*] farewell.

Publications of the
Centre for Reformation and Renaissance Studies

Renaissance and Reformation Texts in Translation:

Lorenzo Valla. *The Profession of the Religious and Selections from The Falsely-Believed and Forged Donation of Constantine.* Trans. O.Z. Pugliese. 2nd ed. (1994), pp. 114

Giovanni Della Casa. *Galateo: A Renaissance Treatise on Manners.* Trans. K. Eisenbichler and K.R. Bartlett. 3rd ed. (1994), pp. 98

Bernardino Ochino. *Seven Dialogues.* Trans. R. Belladonna (1988), pp. 96

Nicholas of Cusa. *The Layman on Wisdom and The Mind.* Trans. M.L. Führer (1989), pp. 112

Andreas Karlstadt, Hieronymous Emser, Johannes Eck. *A Reformation Debate: Karlstadt, Emser, and Eck on Sacred Images.* Trans. B. Mangrum and G. Scavizzi (1998), pp. 115

Whether Secular Government Has the Right to Wield the Sword in Matters of Faith: A Controversy in Nürnberg in 1530. Trans. James M. Estes (1994), pp. 118

Jean Bodin. *On the Demon-Mania of Witches.* Abridged, trans. & ed. R.A. Scott and J.L. Pearl (1995), pp. 219

Tudor and Stuart Texts:

James I. *The True Law of Free Monarchies and Basilikon Doron.* Ed. with an intro. by D. Fischlin and M. Fortier (1996), pp. 181

The Trial of Nicholas Throckmorton. A modernized edition. Ed. with an intro. by Annabel Patterson (1998), pp. 108

Early Stuart Pastoral: The Shepherd's Pipe *by William Browne and others and* The Shepherd's Hunting *by George Wither* Ed. by James Doelman (1999), pp. 196

Occasional Publications:

Register of Sermons Preached at Paul's Cross (1534-1642). Comp. M. MacLure. Revised by P. Pauls and J.C.Boswell (1989), pp. 151

Annotated Catalogue of Early Editions of Erasmus at the Centre for Reformation and Renaissance Studies, Toronto. Comp. J. Glomski and E. Rummel (1994), pp. 153

For additional information, contact:
CRRS Publications, Victoria University, Toronto, Ontario
M5S 1K7, CANADA
(416) 585-4484, fax (416) 585-4579,
e-mail crrs@chass.utoronto.ca